Waltzing Matilda

...and other Australian Yarns

Christina Batey, Linda Ruth Brooks, Julie Cochrane Louise
Elizabeth, Mary Gabb, Jo Hanrahan, Neridah Kentwell,
Marilyn Linn, Jane McLean, Helen Marshall, Victoria Norton,
Rina Robinson, Jo Tregellis, Linda Visman, Pauline Young

Copyright 2014: Christina Batey, Linda Ruth Brooks, Julie Cochrane, Louise Elizabeth, Mary Gabb, Jo Hanrahan, Neridah Kentwell, Marilyn Linn, Jane McLean, Helen Marshall, Victoria Norton, Rina Robinson, Jo Tregellis, Linda Visman, Pauline Young

All rights reserved. Without limiting the rights under copyright reserved above, no part of this work/publication may be reproduced, stored in or introduced into a retrieval system, or transmitted, in any form or by any means (electronic, mechanical, print, photocopying, recording or otherwise), without the prior written permission of the copyright owners.

A copy of this book can be found in the National Library of Australia
Cover Design & artwork by Linda Ruth Brooks
Title page art: 'Down on his luck' by Frederick McCubbin, 1889 (source: collection.artgallery.wa.gov.au) permission {{PD Art}}. This is a public domain image used in accordance with copyright.

ISBN-
Fiction/Family/Romance/Humour/Drama

This book, and others by the authors, can be found at www.amazon.com, online bookstores and other retail outlets.

WaltzingMatilda a work of fiction. Any similarity between the characters in this book and real people, living or dead, is coincidental. By their inclusion here, each author and artist claims and maintains individual copyright of their work/s. Individual contributors are legally liable for their own content; no responsibility is accepted by the publisher. Every attempt has been made by authors to give appropriate acknowledgment for their material, visual or written.

Publisher: *linda ruth brooks publishing*

'Who'll come a-waltzing Matilda with me?'
A. B. 'Banjo' Paterson, 1895

Contents

Waltzing Matilda - Linda Brooks 1

Chook's last day - Louise Elizabeth 13

Murrumbidgee Weekend - Jo Tregellis 17

Quartpot's Hippo - Linda Visman 27

Deliah - Marilyn Linn 32

The No-No Tree - Victoria Norton 34

Trace the shadows - Rina Robinson 38

Camping Under The Bridge - Christina Batey 44

Notoriety Not by Choice - Neridah Kentwell 52

Don't think twice, it'll be Alright! - Mary Gabb 58

The Toy - Marilyn Linn 63

Country Snobs - Linda Brooks 69

I Will Run When Summer Comes - Pauline Young 74

Beatrice Fed the Ducks on Monday - Victoria Norton 75

Black and White - Linda Visman 83

Becoming Country Bumpkins - Julie Cochrane 91

Listening Behind the Door - Louise Elizabeth 96

I am Autumn - Christina Batey 98

The Gold Statue - Mary Gabb 103

Keeping an eye on things - Rina Robinson 107

Preparing for Surgery - Marilyn Linn 113

Two Tiny, Shiny Echidnas - Victoria Norton 118

Sunday School Blues - Linda Brooks 121

Introduction to a Remote Community - Linda Visman.. 126

Suburbia in slumber - Jane McLean 132

A Tremendous Time - Neridah Kentwell...................... 135

Parlez vous francais? - Linda Brooks............................. 140

Birthday Boy - Louise Elizabeth...................................... 143

The Apple Orchard - Helen Marshall 146

First Impressions - Linda Visman 149

The therapist - Mary Gabb 152

The Flood - Louise Elizabeth... 155

The Headland - Victoria Norton 163

Plain Jane - Jane McLean 170

An inconvenient client - Louise Elizabeth.................... 174

Cracker Night at Wombarra Heights - Jo Hanrahan 179

Drawing the Line - Mary Gabb 182

More about Harry - Linda Brooks 187

The Bachelors and Spinsters Ball - Jane McLean............ 189

Hundreds and Thousands - Jo Tregellis 200

Who Stole Christmas? - Linda Brooks.......................... 204

Authors.. 208

Waltzing Matilda

Linda Ruth Brooks

Captain Brentwood wiped rivulets of sweat from his forehead, placed his quill carefully in the worn inkwell, and massaged the cramp in his hand. He deeply regretted the absence of his constable – George Ellerton was an able scribe, and although a little rough around the edges, he at least gave an officer of the law due respect, unlike the locals who had tried his considerable patience that morning.

Looking at the sheaf of papers on his desk, he moaned. Dozens of accounts of the alleged event and not one of them alike.

Although, the circumstances of his investigation hardly warranted the category of 'event'. If in fact it had occurred at all, it would be more correct to call the debacle a tragic incident, unworthy of his rank, but needs must. After all, there had been civil unrest with the shearers.

Will I ever become accustomed to this infernal heat, he thought. After two years I find myself still at the mercy of this penal colony, its wretched humidity, idle convicts, drunkards, thieves and scoundrels—not to mention the wildlife. Damned paperwork, I've been at this nonsense since sunrise. I feel like I've interviewed half the town and I still haven't interviewed the guests from the property.

Who knew a rural farm employed more servants than a Duke's manor and catered for more guests than a royal banquet? If another hired hand tells me that Dagworth Homestead is not a farm, but a substantial sheep station of great importance I will be tempted to lose my cool entirely. And, this from mere servants who object to being called maids. Truly, is there no end to the indignity? I shall be pleased indeed to be back in the city where I know every dangerous street and each shifty villain. Not like this mad country parade of swaggering citizens who seem to delight in leading me a merry dance. So, it only takes one generation for good breeding and high standards to fall by the wayside. Oh, who am I fooling—half of these indigents are probably fresh off the convict ships.

At least in the city he was afforded the respect of his peers, and he had long been inured to the opinions of the criminal element and it mattered little what they thought of him, unless they were armed and faster than he, which was an occasion that had not yet presented itself to Captain Lloyd Brentwood, lately of Brisbane and soon to return there. Post haste if he had his way. But fate did not appear to be smiling on his dearest wishes. With the way things were going, he would be held up for a week, instead of the few hours the incident required.

'Who's left Menzies?' he called to the casually dressed constable who was deep in conversation with the garrulous publican who more than likely had no connection to the event, but insisted that he had 'information of great import and don't mind 'ow long I waits ter see the gentleman city officer'. Realising that he himself was in danger of losing his manners, Captain Brentwood added, 'If you please, Constable Menzies, could you bring me the list of relevant persons, and if refreshments are available I wonder if you could procure me some lunch. Also, while I have your attention, it would be indeed beneficial if you could spare me the time to peruse the names with me and inform me of the connection of the person to the ... er ... case. I don't want to waste my time speaking with individuals with the merest connection to events or those who have heard whisperings from cousins twice-removed.'

Loosening the top button of his military coat, he rose and walked to the dusty window that overlooked the street. Drovers leant on the doorway to the Public House, tankards held loosely in that casual manner he had come to know that belied innate alertness. Several men pulled their hats forward, avoiding his scrutiny, amusement etched on their faces. Hearing soft footfalls he turned. The publican had entered the room.

'If it would please yer, sir, I'd be mighty pleased to shout y'good self a meal at my Public 'ouse across the road, and I c'd tell yer me tale—er—version of the events pertaining to the night in question.' This statement was accompanied by a broad toothless smile. 'Beg yer pardon, sir, I'm Harry Garrett, business man and owner of the local...'

'I'm sorry, Mr Garrett, but I am not accustomed to conducting matters of military investigation in public places, no offence to your establishment, of course. However, I will confer with the constable and call for you if I require a statement,' said Captain Brentwood.

Harry shuffled his red-brown hat with earnest hands, while attempting to smooth some stray strands of hair over his bald crown.

'However, I do thank you for the cordial offer of your hospitality. It just wouldn't suit. Protocol, you know.'

'Oh, of course, sir, silly of me ter...ah, we 'ave a more relaxed attitude 'ere in the country, but I sees yer intention, indeed I do. I'd be well pleased if yer'd accept a meal brought over. I'll jest get Molly to bring you a lamb roast with veg'tables.'

'I'll pay,' said Captain Brentwood, ignoring the look that passed between the publican and the constable.

Half an hour later, Captain Brentwood regretted his request for Constable Menzies to join him. Instead of a briefing on those connected to the situation, he had been regaled with what he could only call 'gossip'. And that summation was definitely charitable. The constable had taken the opportunity to fill the captain in on local unrest, the political implications of the shearers grievances, which would have been annoying at any time, but was made all the more discomforting because the ebullient man had sought responses to his verbose expostulations and Captain Brentwood did not like to be interrupted when partaking of a meal. To the captain's surprise the repast was superior in every way.

'So Menzies, what you're saying is that I should see everyone on this list?' Captain Brentwood's patience was wearing thin.

Constable Menzies smiled. 'Oh, alright. But who's this Banjo Patterson fellow? What sort of a name is Banjo? I've never seen such a parade of time-wasting...'

'He's a poet, Captain.'

'A *what*?'

'A poet, sir. Aye, I'll admit he's not what one usually expects of a poet. He writes bush ballads. He's not of the style of that poncy poet Lord Byron, of course, but in these parts ... well the whole nation really, he's considered somewhat of a celebrity. Very popular fellow...'

Captain Brentwood's eyes narrowed. Was the constable deliberately baiting him? Would like day never end? Rising to his feet in what he hoped what a dismissive manner he said, 'And when may we reasonably expect this 'Banjo' chap to grace us with his presence?'

'Well, er...' The constable squirmed. 'It's hard to say, sir. I hear he's presently engaged in assisting the town Reverand choose a right piece of horseflesh at the local saleyard.'

'Oh, never mind. Is anyone waiting...' Seeing the constable stumble for a response, Captain Brentwood strode across the room, 'Don't worry, Menzies, I'll see to them myself.'

Brentwood scanned the long corridor. There, on an array of chairs, was what could only be described as a veritable crowd of people. A lively crowd at that. His writing hand cramped with dread. Taking a deep breath he began the interviews. Life in his Mother country, where gaining information was akin to pulling teeth, had not prepared the captain for a noisy mob of people from all walks of life eagerly waiting to offer their statements.

'Well, it was well on nigh over a year ago,' said Mrs Argeton, the cook from Dagwood Homestead, 'if one listened to local rumour, and I must make it clear that I am not one of those idle gossipy women, it would appear that some poor fellow drowned himself out at the Combo Waterhole. There are others that have a different view, of course. Why Harry Garrett over at The Drover's Arm would be your best source for all the variations... Have you met our publican?'

'Yes, Madam, I have had the ... er ... pleasure just this morning. However, I am trying to separate the facts from fiction and innuendo.'

'Oh Lordy,' laughed Mrs Argeton, 'you sound like that poet fella with those big words. And don't stand on ceremony with me, young man, I'm known as Mrs around here. We've no truck with airs and graces.'

'Right. Certainly Mrs Argeton. So can you tell me anything that you saw or witnessed first-hand?'

'Oh Captain, I never laid eyes on any of that nonsense. Why isn't it my place to be in the kitchen? I'm lucky enough to see the inside of m'own house in daylight with all the work I do. Not that I'm complaining mind you, the Macpherson's are a lovely family. Why, Mrs Macpherson even gave me the day off with pay to come in here to help.'

'She did *what*?'

'For sure, and wasn't I just tellin' you so?' Mrs Argeton leaned forward, her eyes clouded.

Captain Brentwood paused before speaking again. 'So, the only thing you can tell me is that this incident of the shearers' strike and the burning of the shearing shed occurred a year ago?'

'Why, Captain, never did I say such a thing. It was a year ago that Mr Paterson visited with the Macpherson family. The fire that destroyed the shed happened months before, in September, the beginning of spring.'

'And what does the visit of Mr Paterson have to do with anything?'

Mrs Argeton bristled. 'I don't know that I understand your

meaning. Mr Paterson was a guest.'

'Was he present at the time of the fire?'

'I don't know all the comings and goings of guests. I'm told how many people will require meals. Sometimes I know who is there, but often I don't.'

'But you know about the visit in January of 1894?'

'Well, yes, there was great excitement. That was when Mr Paterson wrote a wonderful poem. He called it 'Waltzing Matilda'. Miss Christina remembered a piece of music she'd heard while she was in Victoria. Mr Paterson was quite taken with the music and worked his poem to set with it. So it's not just a poem really, but a true bush ballad, and if I'm not mistaken it will become quite as famous as Mr Paterson's other writing. There's...'

'Mrs Argeton, I would implore you to stick to the facts in hand. I am here to investigate the death of Samuel Hoffmeister who allegedly set fire to the woolshed at the homestead. They tell me he was known as "French" or "Frenchy".'

'Well, why didn't you say so? What would I be knowing about the shearers, for don't they have their own quarters and shearer's cook? I don't know anything about that. Can I take my leave, now?'

Captain Brentwood sighed. 'Yes, of course, Mrs Argeton.'

'Menzies!' he shouted. The constable scurried into the room, giving the captain the distinct impression he'd been listening at the door.

'Yes, sir.'

'Could you please take another look at *your* list, and send away those with no knowledge of the night in question.'

'Do you want me to interview them first, Captain?'

'Of course not.'

'Then how am I to ascertain whether they know anything about the death of Mr Hoffmeister?'

'Well, at least get me the doctor who signed the death certificate.'

'That's not possible, Captain. Old Doc Parsons died nigh on six months ago now. Fond of a tipple he was. Liver got him in the end.'

'The records?'

'Well here's the thing. That's just as much a mystery as the dead man. There must have been a death certificate – or that's what we assumed, but no-one has ever been able to turn one up.'

The afternoon progressed in a most unsatisfactory fashion. Menzies had perused the list and only dismissed one person.

The owner of Dagworth Homestead was an affable chap who volunteered a gratutitous amount of information about sheep farming and the superior quality of Australian wool. 'Our country lives on the sheep's back, Captain,' he said. 'But I know nothing about Samuel Hoffmeister's death. He's buried here in town, I know that much. He was one of my shearers, surly sort of fellow. Fond of a bit of biffo, especially after a night at the public house. I was busy attending to the fire. Terrible blow that was – watching the shed burn down, hearing the sheep – not able to do much more than form a line with half a dozen metal buckets. No farmer likes to see his animals suffer like that, even if it's necessary to sendsome to the slaughter house. Cruel end for them.'

'I'm afraid you are rather veering from the point, sir.'

'I'm trying to say that not everyone can take living here. The shearers can be a belligerent lot. It's a shocking thing when men burn down a woolshed that provides their livelihood. It's a harsh country, that it is, Captain. There's none of your hedgerows and thatched cottages with rose gardens blooming all year 'round and greenery for miles like you're used to – it's dusty and windblown, red dust at that. Near chokes a man. If there isn't a drought where the ground is too parched for a solitary blade of grass, there's a deluge that washes the sheep and all in it's wake. Then there's the bushfires. You don't know despair until you've seen these things, Captain. Australia, land of extremes. But I guess you know that – been here a while have you?'

'I fail to see how the geography, or the weather has anyting to do with the death of Samual Hoffmeister, and I find your attitude less than helpful. I am an officer of the Crown investigating a death. If you have nothing to enlighten me on the matter at hand I will take up no more of your time, sir.'

Captain Brentwood damped down his frustration. He hadn't wanted to come to Winton, but a soldier didn't question his superiors. Over a year had passed since the burning of the wooldshed and the death of Hoffmeister. If the truth was hidden – there was little prospect of it coming to light.

When questioned, Menzies informed the captain that the troopers who were rumoured to have pursued the hapless Hoffmeister had all vowed they were together on the night and were miles from Winton, checking into a report of a bank holdup by bushrangers. There was even a scrawled entry in the police records. Two of the troopers had returned to England and the other had been posted to 'somewhere in the Northern Territory'.

The head shearer had nothing to offer – he was newly appointed, and the shearers quarters were empty – the itinerent workers were working at other employment, most likely as jackaroos, logging or working on the railways. The shearer's mechanic was not available. He was only in town during the shearing season, which was over for the year.

The new doctor who had taken over Doc Parsons office was

more than willing to see the captain, but he declared that there was no record that Hoffmeister had ever been a patient, much less information on the man's death.

The sons of the owner of Dagworth Homestead were relaxed, casual fellows who spoke with much bravado of their terrible tussle with death and destruction fighting the fire in the huge woolshed.

Captain Brentwood was weary. The constable had just brought him a tankard of ale when he heard a melodic female voice. A fashionable lady strode into the room. She appeared to be in her early twenties, and smelt of soap and fresh flowers. Flicking her gloves off quickly she gave the captain a brisk handshake. 'I'm Christina Macpherson,' she said, and sat in the chair opposite the desk without waiting for an invitation. 'Am I the last person you need to interview?'

'I wouldn't say need…' The Captain sighed. 'But no, I still have to see that poet fellow.'

'Oh Barty, you'll like him.'

'Barty? I thought his name was Banjo.'

'That's just the name he writes under – he chose it because of a racehorse, you know. His name is Andrew Barton Paterson.'

The captain raised a quizzical eyebrow.

Christina continued, 'He listened to a song I played and wrote a poem for it. Did you know that? It's been published in the papers and it will be made into sheet music soon. It's marvellous.'

There was an artlessness about the woman. Her eyes lit up with the telling of the tale. In spite of himself, Captain Brentwood found himself overtaken with curiosity.

'Does he write many songs? I thought he was a poet?'

'Oh, Barty is much more than a poet. He was a practising solicitor – I think he began writing in his student days. But this bush ballad, 'Waltzing Matilda' is the first one set to music.' Her smile was beautiful. The captain found himself smiling in return.

'But you don't want me to go on about that. I must warn you that I shall be of no use whatsoever to you. I was in Melbourne at the time of the fire in the great woolshed. Barty wasn't here either, he travels prodigously, much the same way as he writes.'

'You are refreshing Miss Christina, you're the first to admit that you don't have any information to assist the investigation.'

'Oh dear, not much happens here in the country – *usually*. I s'pose you've had every gossip in town bending your ear.'

'In the interest of discretion I won't comment.' The captain leaned back in his chair and smiled. 'So this 'ballad' – it's a Waltz tune...?'

'Oh no,' laughed Christina, 'The song is about a swagman – they're out-of-work fellows travelling all over looking for work. The swaggie in the song steals a sheep, and rather than be taken in by troopers he jumps into the billabong and drowns.'

The captain laughed, 'Not a romance then.'

'Not at all. Other than the romance of the land. Barty has a wonderful way of conveying Australian life.'

'So why call it 'Waltzing Matilda? You must forgive a humble soldier – I have only been in the Australia for two years, and seldom in rural areas.'

'Oh dear, I'm sorry, I'm not explaining it very well. "Waltzing" refers to travelling on foot with all of one's possessions, which describes the life of the swaggie, and "Matilda" is the Australian word for whatever he uses to carry his belongings.'

Captain Brentwood's brow furrowed. 'Hmm, I would like to say "I see", but quite frankly I don't. Although, I should very much like to hear you sing it.'

'Well, don't expect to be any the wiser when you hear the song,' said Christina. 'Are you going to offer me a drink? I'm parched...Oh there's Barty now.' She pointed out the window to where a tall man with enviable grace was dismounting from a magnificent stallion. Andrew Barton Paterson was lean and tanned. In no manner did he fit the image Captain Brentwood had formed. As if aware of their scrutiny, Paterson turned and gazed through hooded eyes, tipped his hat and headed into the public house. Men swarmed around him with backslapping greetings.

Christina smiled at the astonishment on the captain's face. 'You don't really expect him to come in for an interview do you? He's not one to waste anyone's time – his own included. After all, he only wrote a whimsical poem, even if some claim that it's a political allegory.' She eyed the captain with barely concealed amusement. 'Although he's tremendously popular, Barty's not one to dance to any man's tune. Comes of being a nationalist, I suppose.'

'Well, it's a good thing to have an upstanding subject of King and Country.'

'Oh, Captain Brentwood. Barty's nation is *Australia*.'

---

*'Waltzing Matilda' is Australia's best known bush ballad and is often referred to as 'the unofficial national anthem of Australia'.

Chook's last day

Louise Elizabeth

The day was dull. Grey clouds dampened our mood until a younger brother raced up the stairs, breathless with news. 'The chicken man's coming.'

'Wow. When?'

'Soon. I heard Mum talking to Mrs Green about it.'

We crept downstairs. Fearful of being sent away from the action, we tried to make ourselves invisible. Mum was standing in the laundry, chatting with her friend when we heard the side gate open. We peered out the kitchen window as the man with one tooth shuffled down the path. He wore a faded blue singlet roughly tucked into a pair of grey trousers, fraying where they met his boots.

'Hello Missus. How many today?'

Mum held up two fingers. 'Thanks, Tom.'

She looked around quickly to ensure we were out of sight.

'Don't worry,' her friend encouraged. 'The children are upstairs.'

We stifled giggles as we sneaked down the hallway and silently crept up the railing to get to the mandarin tree whose branches reach across the verandah roof. My older brother climbed up first and then reached down to help his siblings. We slid along the tin until we had a good view of the backyard.

Mum handed the man an axe. 'Let me know when you're finished, Tom.'

She and her friend retreated far away from the sight of death. We could hear them talking in the kitchen as they made themselves a drink.

Tom leisurely grabbed a chook and held it by its legs. Its wings flapped as it squawked. He threw the hapless bird over the wood chopping block and in a flash the axe came down and the chook's head fell to the ground. Tom dropped the body on the grass and then chased and caught another hen. It was killed the same way.

I watched in horror as visions from the Scarlett Pimpernel came to mind. I looked around but there were no old women knitting, just the headless chooks running in circles until they dropped. I thought I was going to be sick. I wriggled back from the edge of the roof and climbed down.

Once we were all on the ground, the boys raced out the back to inspect the corpses. Mum yelled at us to come inside but she was ignored. Tom grabbed a headless chook and holding its body firm on the chopping block, sliced off its feet.

'Here boys have some fun with these.'

He demonstrated how to pull the tendons and make the claws move. Mum stomped over and grabbed the feet from my brothers.

'I'll take these.'

She threw the offending items in the garbage bin and glared at Tom who appeared embarrassed at her reaction. He shuffled over, accepted his money and slinked down the pathway.

'Now play like decent children.'

Mum joined her friend inside.

I sat on the swing, riding back and forth, going higher and higher. My older brother grabbed the chain causing me to lose my balance and get off. I stood up indignant at my treatment and my younger brothers' sniggering. I turned to glare at them.

No sooner was my back to my older brother than I felt a tickle on my neck. I whipped around and saw him holding chicken feet which were opening and closing. I ran screaming away only to be confronted by my younger brothers each holding a similar disgusting item. I didn't know which way to turn. My siblings found it very amusing. I felt sick and trapped and was never so glad to see my mother.

'Stop that.'

Her voice echoed past the wood pile to my brothers who hesitated but continued their tormenting. I continued my screaming. A neighbour came in, took in the situation and grabbed my older brother and deftly removed the feet from his hands.

'Go and wash the blood off. Not a very manly way to behave.'

Shame-faced, my brother slunk into the laundry to cleanse his hands. My younger brothers dropped their treasures on the ground, flinging a 'sorry' over their shoulders and followed their leader inside. I fell to the ground sobbing.

'There's no need to go overboard.' My mother's friend's dry voice was unsympathetic. 'We get you're upset.'

I glared at her and went inside to continue my isolation from my disgusting siblings. Adults are so cruel, so insensitive.

Murrumbidgee Weekend

Jo Tregellis

It was time for the annual October long weekend get-together. Robert and his mates, Jim and Harry, had arrived at the site after work late on Friday afternoon. This year it was their turn to clear away rubbish and set up the communal tent which served as a dining shelter and meeting point.

'Not too bad this time, only one bag of rubbish,' Robert said as he pulled the drawstring tight on the large plastic bag, his muscles only hinting at his great strength.

'Good.' Jim had begun to drive the stakes into the ground. 'Boy, the ground's dry. Damn drought. It makes everything hard work, but it won't beat me.'

'Yeah, no sign of rain. Must be six months or more since we had a drop. The river's pretty low, waist high. I hope it's enough for riding tubes.'

'Come on, put your muscles into it.' Harry laughed as he unrolled the canvas and ropes and spread them out, carefully checking each one. His deep voice spurred them on. In fifteen minutes the shelter was up. 'We'll get the gas bottles off the Ute now and set up the barbeque and hot water. Neil and Barbara are bringing a gas fridge and Bill's got a new generator for lighting.'

'We'll be all set then,' said Robert. After dusk they sat under the dining shelter enjoying a beer, sleeping bags ready for the night. 'In the morning, we'll go down to the river bank and get a log to burn through tomorrow night. The kids love to make toast over an open fire.'

Robert woke the others at six. Sunlight speckled the treetops and the dew released scent from the eucalypts. Robert breathed it all in. It was such a relief to be out of the office for three days. He was one of the accountants in town and apart from all the usual clients, the farmers and graziers kept him busy.

'Track's grown over a bit.' Jim's hiking boots trampled the grass like mini bulldozers. 'The mob will soon wear it down, but. My two boys inherited my feet. Thank goodness the girls are like their mother.'

Jim and his wife Annette ran the small supermarket in the west of the town. There's no competition in that area so they had been doing well, as Jim was first to admit. He never said anything but Robert knew that Jim had photos of six sponsored black kids in the sunroom. They were placed with photos of his own children.

'What about you, Jim? Business okay still?' Robert asked.

'Well, to tell you the truth, no. Most orders are put on the slate now. Poor buggers can't pay but we know they will when the drought breaks. We have to hang on until then.'

The brown water of the 'Bidgee flowed past them. Because the level was low the smell of earth and ochre came up to the men.

'Smells good, eh? Sort of old and new at the same time.' Harry stretched his wiry arms up above his sandy hair. 'Wouldn't be dead for quids, eh?' Harry arrived from Queensland seven years ago with a swag on his back, the colour of the sky in his eyes and empty pockets. Neil and Barbara had given him a start as a jackeroo on their sheep property but soon found out that he was a great cook and now the shearers sing his praises every season.

'Is your partner coming today, Harry?' Robert was a little curious because Harry and Sue had two small children but didn't live together.

'Yeah, Sue's coming and the littlies. I reckon me boy Josh will be big enough to come in the tyre tube this year.' Harry kicked up a heap of twigs and leaves. 'What do you think of this log for the campfire?'

'Looks fine, Harry.'

They carried the log back and set it down in the cleared space heaping twigs all around it and in its hollows.

'Better light it about eleven. It should be glowing well by tonight. Think I'll put up our tent so Annette can unpack straight into it. It's starting to warm up too.' Jim put his battered slouch hat over his curly black hair.

By noon on Saturday everyone except Neil had arrived. The camp was a very busy place. Later that afternoon they went down to the riverbank. The muddy brown water shone, burnished by the sun. Trees overhung it, grasses crept up to it, red soil lined it, water birds called it home and its bends beckoned the inquisitive. The crowd always came to this spot. It had a gentle slope to access the river and lots of shade. Annette and Sue sat massaging their feet in the coarse sand. Sue's youngest child, Hannah, was not yet walking but Josh at four was a handful. 'I spend a lot of my time runnin' around after Josh. He's so quick. Probably be good at athletics when he's older.'

'My boys are too heavy for athletics. Jim's a big man. They're all into the footy. Jim's the coach of the junior team. I just love when it's my turn to wash all the jerseys.' Annette pulled a face. 'Oh, I don't really mind.'

Robert cupped his hands around his mouth and called out,

'Tyre tube rides down the river will start in ten minutes. The ride will stop at Bushy Bend and Bill will pick you up in the ute and trailer and bring you back here. Thanks for that Bill. Who's first? One grown-up and two children per ride.'

Robert was a great organiser. You could tell he enjoyed it.

'Now, you know that the water slows at Bushy Bend and becomes shallow enough on the left bank to stand up and take the tube to the shore. Then you throw it in the trailer and come back with Bill. Two turns today if we have time. Okay, enjoy yourselves!' He went off to see about the evening BBQ.

Harry explained to Josh that people had to be very careful when they were playing in the river.

'Why, Dad?'

'Well, there might be things hidden under the water or sticking out of it that could hurt us.'

'What Dad?'

'Well, old trees and branches, sometimes machinery and rubbish and even animals. All these things are called snags and we have to look out for them.'

'Mummy gives me snags to eat. Are sausages snags too, Dad?'

'Yes, son.'

'Why, Dad.'

'Dunno, son.'

'Where's the tube come from, Dad?'

'From inside a big tractor tyre.'

'How does it get blowed up Dad?'

'The same way that we put air in the car tyres.'

Josh nodded. 'I can't touch that air thing, can I, Dad?'

'No, Josh. That thing's called a valve. C'mon it's our turn.'

'Hannah coming Dad?'

'No, Hannah's too little, mate. You're a big boy now.'

'I'm coming with you and your Dad.' Bill's boy Sam was eight and he had done all this before. 'Ya just need ta hold on real tight and push ya legs straight out in front.'

'Let's go!' Harry shoved off and jumped in. The current took them off quickly. Sam and Josh were yelling with excitement. Up and down and round and round. Dizzy trees, flickering sun, great globules of water over them and in five thrilling minutes the swirling, twirling ride was over.

'Wow! That was so cool.' Sam shouted.

'So cool,' echoed Josh.

When they got back the hot plate was full of sizzly, juicy sausages, lamb chops, onions and tomatoes. Robert had everyone in orderly lines, plates in hand. 'Salad and bread on the table near Annette. Find a spot in the shelter.' He sat down for a breather. A few magpies arrived to share the time. Treetops swished softly. Two small boats with outboard motors putted by.

'Prob'ly after cod if the bloody carp haven't taken over completely. How about a carp-catching competition tomorrow?'

'Hooray!' shouted the kids.

'Adults are included,' Robert announced.

'I've got five dollars for the winner,' Jim said as he flourished the note in the air.

'I'll match it,' said Bill. 'Hey, look. There's something floating down the river.'

'What is it?'

'Is it a body?'

'Is it big?

'Is it a bunyip?'

All these questions came tumbling out as they rushed to find a vantage point.

'No, it's a cow. Probably drowned trying to get a drink of water from the river. It's been dead for a while. It's all bloated. There's nothing we can do.'

Evening crept in and night followed. Lights and lanterns shone on the games of cards, dominoes, scrabble and snakes and ladders.

'Lights out at ten thirty,' Robert announced. We've got a busy day tomorrow.' On Sunday morning, Robert had breakfast with Barbara. 'I hope Neil comes this afternoon.'

'Me too,' Barbara replied. 'Shame his weekend was shortened but when you stand a stud merino ram, things have to happen when they have to happen. Besides if we didn't have *Bidgee Beau* we'd be broke by now with this damn drought.'

'It is bad, I know,' said Robert not mentioning money. 'Forecasters are saying there won't be any rain until March.'

'God help us,' Barbara sighed. 'Come on. Let's get ready for fishing.'

All the entrants were assembled. 'If you catch a fish that is not a carp would you please get Harry to identify it and decide whether or not you can keep it for tonight's dinner.'

'Yes, Robert,' chorused the kids.

The whoosh and click of rods and reels and little squeals of laughter filled the air. Jim was first. 'I've hooked something.' He began to reel in, making faces and flexing muscles as if he was landing a bronze whaler. The fish came out of the water. A big fat carp.

'Good on yer Jim.' Everyone cheered. Jim hit the carp on the head and threw it in the hole dug especially for that purpose. After two hours, fifteen carp were in that hole. Bill caught a female Murray Cod, which he put back in the river. The edible catch was disappointingly small, two silver perch and three catfish. 'Yuk, they're ugly.' The girls giggled. 'Look at those big whiskers. I bet they must be ticklish.'

Jim won the competition and gave the kids two dollars each.

'Wow, thanks Jim.' They pranced around holding high their golden coins.

Neil arrived about six o'clock and brought his guitar with him and a noisy sing-a-long later rose up to a veiled moon and stars.

Suddenly, over the top of the din, Sue screamed. 'I can't find my kids.'

'What do you mean, you can't find them?'

'I don't know where they are. They're gone.'

'Why weren't you watching them?' Harry snapped.

'I thought I knew where they were. Hannah was asleep in her pram and Josh was dancing around to the music. The pram's gone as well.' Sue scowled at Harry. 'Anyway why can't you watch them sometimes? I have to do everything.'

Robert interrupted. 'This is just wasting time.' He began to direct teams to search in key areas. 'Bill, you and Sam go down the track to Bushy Bend. Neil and Jim go down to the water and follow the bank around. Stay here with the children, please Annette.'

Sue ran from Harry, shouting 'Josh, Josh.'

'Wait Sue, wait for me, I've got the torches.' Harry raced after her.

Sue didn't know which way to turn. She ran in zigzag pattern.

'Please, God, please don't take them from me.' Sue's eyes were wide and desperate. Her heart thudded. She tripped, sprawling over into the rough sand. Her forehead hit something hard. 'Oh dear God. It's Hannah's rattle.'

Harry shouted, 'There's the pram on the bank.'

Sue got up and ran towards Harry's voice.

Harry's knees went weak. He barely made it to the pram. His mouth was dry. My little girl. What if she isn't in the pram? Oh no, what'll I bloody do without my kids? Unnerving thoughts bombarded his brain. His voice pierced the darkness. 'I promise I'll look after them better and their Mum. Please God don't let them be dead.' He shone the torch into the pram. Hannah was there. Harry clutched her to his chest.

Sue reached Harry. He thrust the baby into her arms. She felt Hannah's warmth. 'Thank you God, thank you.'

'Take Hannah back to camp. 'I have to find our son.'

Harry was deciding which way to go when he realised, 'The bloody tube's gone.' Across his mind flashed a vision of police dragging the river with a net. 'No, no. I won't let that happen. Josh, Josh,' he screamed. 'I'm coming. Dad's coming.' Harry's gut was hurting. Branches hit his head. Twigs and sharp rocks stabbed his legs. 'What's that ahead? Jim, Neil?'

'Yes, mate, we're here. We checked the baby and continued our search.'

'Hannah's okay but the bloody tractor tube is missing.'

'Bloody hell.'

The three men instinctively shone their torches out on the water. Nothing. They pushed on calling. Nothing. Harry's gut twisted into a frantic knot.

'Bugger, how much further to Bushy Bend do ya reckon, eh?'

'About six minutes.'

'That's too long. Move faster.'

Coming to a slight bend Jim called 'Coo-ee.'

'Coo-ee,' came back through the night. A lantern swayed ahead. Sam stood in the clearing. 'Dad told me to wait for you. We called to Josh and we think we heard him answer from further downstream. Dad's on his way.'

'That's great. Good lad.'

Jim was about to suggest that he return to camp and drive a vehicle back when they heard the sound of a motor. Robert had anticipated the need.

'We must keep going. Take turns in calling.' Three hundred metres on they thought they heard a faint voice. 'Josh, Josh, is that you?'

'Dad, Dad, Daddy.'

The men nodded to each other unable to speak for a few seconds.

'Where are you son?'

'Tube, Dad. I'm in the tube.'

Harry walked into the river, the others close behind. 'Shine your torches downstream. There he is.' Half wading, half swimming, half laughing, half crying, Harry reached the tube.

'Josh, I've got you.' Harry held him tight.

'Dad, the tube got stuck. Is it a snag?'

'Yes son, it's a snag. The tube's caught on branches under the water. There isn't enough water to cover them.'

'Shh. Hear that hissing. Another couple of minutes and this tube will be airless.' Neil spoke softly.

'Hell.'

Harry stroked his son's head, his tears hidden in all the wetness.

'Climb onto my shoulders, son.'

'Dad. Hannah watched me. I'm a big boy.

Quartpot's Hippo

Linda Visman

We called the place 'Quartpot's Camp'. The buildings had only been there for about a year, and us whitefellas hadn't yet got used to calling it by its real name. Most of us couldn't get our tongues around it anyway.

The tiny outstation community was about three hundred kilometres out from Alice Springs over the red-dirt highway. When he'd first been granted his claim to this living area, Quartpot had installed a bore and an elevated water tank. These now overlooked a tin shed and two new besser-brick, iron-roofed houses. The old man and his wife lived in one of the houses, along with their daughter and her family. The other housed a son and more extended family.

Where the spinifex grass had been cleared under the sparse-leafed trees beside the houses, stood a couple of bough shelters. Built from rough forked uprights and cross-members, and covered with leafy branches, they were great places to relax, away from the oven-like house interiors. Quartpot's family would play interminable card games there, whiling away the hot summer days. If you looked out to the surrounding bush, you'd see the remains of the humpies they lived in before the houses were built.

Unlike most people in remote settlements, the old man had a

vegetable garden. This added an air of respectability to the otherwise junk-strewn, dust-blown community. A couple of Holden Kingswoods sat where they'd died, providing spare parts for the next acquisition. There was often no vehicle to take people to the cattle station store, thirty kilometres away, or the kids to the little classroom at Ross's Camp, another outstation ten kilometres in the other direction.

About a dozen kids lived at Quartpot's camp, ranging in age from ten years down to babes in arms. Seven were of school age, and their grandfather was very keen they attend school. He believed you could always get what you wanted if you knew how the system operated – and you couldn't know this if you didn't get an education.

The main school for the area, with two classrooms, was in a community about forty-five kilometres away. Teachers also travelled to three remote classrooms each day in departmentally provided Toyota troop carriers. I was the teacher at Ross's Camp, the outstation classroom that Quartpot's family attended. I had to drive right by his place to get there, so I always stopped to pick up the kids on the way.

On this particular day when I drove into the camp, they weren't ready. That wasn't unusual; nobody got them moving until they saw my Toyota coming. Most were still eating breakfast. They all needed to wash the sleep from their eyes and the dirt from their faces. While waiting for them, I wandered over to where Quartpot tended a campfire outside his house. As in all the outstations, they had no electricity, and cooking was done outside in the traditional way. Kangaroo, bush turkey and goanna were roasted in fire-pits or just tossed onto the fire. Damper and wild roots were cooked in the hot sand and ashes. Chief among the few modern conveniences was the billycan.

This day, the old man was carefully stirring the contents of a large, blackened billy. From it wafted an aroma that made my mouth water.

'Morning, Quartpot. How are you today?'

'Ah, good morning, Teacha. Good, good. Kids not be long.' His smile, behind a grey-streaked beard, revealed tobacco-stained teeth. The two front ones were completely missing, knocked out at his man-making, many years before. He patted the ground. 'Come, sit down.'

'Thanks.' I nodded at the billy. 'What are you cooking?'

'I make stew.' He rubbed his skinny tummy. 'Good tucker this one.'

'What's in it? Smells wonderful.'

'Some meat, vegetable from garden – carrot, potato.'

'There must be something else in there. It doesn't smell familiar.'

The old man picked up a red foil package from the ground where he'd tossed it.

'This one 'ere. Make it taste real good.'

I read the label. French Onion Soup. I grinned.

'Well, You'll have to invite me to dinner one day, Quartpot. If it tastes as good as it smells, then it's better than anything I've ever cooked.'

A couple of girls, three or four years old, came and sat by the fire, peeping up at me through hair that had hardly ever seen a comb. I smiled at them and they giggled. I turned back to the billy.

'What kind of meat do you use, Quartpot? Kangaroo?'

He glanced at the girls, then at me, a serious look on his face – though his eyes twinkled under the bushy eyebrows.

'No, not kangaroo. Hippopotamus.'

'Hippopotamus! You're joking.'

He chuckled. 'No, true. That hippopotamus, he make real good stew.'

'Teacha! We ready!'

The kids had opened the doors of the troopie and were climbing into the back.

'Okay. Better go, I suppose. See you later, Quartpot. Enjoy your stew!'

I walked towards the troopie.

'Okay kids, how many for school today?'

We all counted, one, two, three, four, five, six.

'Who's missing? Must be Gary. Where is he?'

'Gone to store,' said one of the older girls. 'Him got no trouser – it got big hole.'

'Okay. Let's go. The others will think we're not coming.'

The wide front seat was taken up with boxes of fruit, boiled eggs, long-life juice and milk. With the store so far away, the kids would have nothing to eat all day if I didn't take this food with me. A remote area allowance paid for it, the parents signing over the money to the school, so a decent feed was available at least four days a week.

Once the youngsters were all sitting on the bench seats in the back of the vehicle, we set off. I drove through the deep, though now dry, river crossing and headed across the floodplain towards school. A long, spreading plume of pink dust trailed behind us, and the shock-absorbers got their usual heavy workout on the rough dirt road.

I kept an eye open. We were on the local cattle station, which extended forty or fifty kilometres in every direction, and there were no fences. The bore trough wasn't far off the road, which meant we were quite likely to run into cattle – though not literally, I hoped. Seven-year-old Charlie the Chatterbox, in the seat just behind me, nattered on about his weekend activities. Suddenly, his arm shot out over my shoulder, nearly taking my ear off. 'Look, Teacha, look. Hippopotamus!'

I corrected my involuntary jerk at the wheel and forced my heart back down out of my throat. 'What? Hippopotamus? Where?'

'Ober dere, see? Brown one.'

I looked 'ober dere'. The only brown thing I could see was a steer, pulling at a bit of green feed that the recent rain had teased from the red dirt. A steer that belonged to the cattle station. Suddenly, light dawned, and I couldn't help laughing out loud.

Charlie had just made it clear what the meat in Quartpot's billy really was, and where it had come from. The old rogue! He'd told the kids that the animals were hippos so they wouldn't accidentally let on that he was pinching steers from the station.

And now I also understood why the kids had always looked at me strangely when I tried to teach the English words 'little' and 'big'. The picture I used to illustrate the concepts just happened to be of a little bird on a big hippopotamus.

Author's note: This story is based on real people, places and events

Deliah

Marilyn Linn

Drab, grey clouds hung low, breathing heavily. Slow moving people gather in small groups under the cover of the wide verandah. Flashes of colour break the monotony of the dark suits of men as the women wrap up against the chilly wind, still shivering.

A new arrival is surreptitiously scanned by the clots of people looking for recognition. A quiet word, a slight nod and occasional hug as someone is welcomed into a group. Feet shuffle, going nowhere, like chained elephants.

A restless murmur ripples through the gathering as they wait to be invited to the inner sanctum. 'Ladies and Gentlemen, will you please come on in and take your seats.'

Obediently the bland-faced people move through the open glass doors and find their way inside. Mutterings rise and fall as people find a seat which suits them. Last ones in get what's left.

The pious-faced celebrant takes his place as the rostrum. 'Ladies and Gentlemen...'

I expect to hear him say '...we are gathered today to join this man and this woman in Holy Matrimony...' but he doesn't. I am jolted back to reality.

'We are gathered today to celebrate the life of Mrs Deliah

Parslow...'

I hadn't known Mrs Parslow well, but I knew her daughter, Cassy, and was there for her sake. In all, there were about fifty people in the chapel, all looking like they had somewhere else to be. A hush falls over the assembly and for a long moment no-one speaks.

I see the attendant go to the discrete control box and twiddle a knob. A furnace blast of loud music shatters the dullness. Trumpets blare in ear-shattering revelry. The Parslows were all reggae music fans and this funeral is going to get moving. A local band of music-makers dance up the aisles, inviting people to join them. Some do and much laughter ensues.

After a handful of minutes the music calms down and the more serious side of the ceremony is dealt with. Outside the rain pelts down but just as the casket is lowered, a brilliant ray of sunshine breaks through the overhead glass panels and shines on the coffin of Mrs Deliah Parslow. I know in that moment her soul is free.

Again the reggae band take over, encouraging everyone to clap their hands and sway their bodies to the rhythm as we try to sing the Lord's Prayer with reggae accompaniment.

A moment of quiet reflection is given before the band has the congregation on its feet, dancing into the adjoining lounge for refreshments and entertainment.

What a send-off! The old lady would have loved it.

The No-No Tree

Victoria Norton

Evelyn remembered watching her two younger sisters as they danced on the lawn. Wearing brightly coloured swimming costumes with short white pleated skirts, the girls practiced gymnastics – standing on each other and striking poses. It was as if they were listening to an invisible orchestra playing music only they could hear. They were like butterflies flitting over a flower bed in springtime, foot-light and dainty.

So much time had passed since then, and yet the pang of

nostalgia bit hard. Evelyn held the birthday card, not sure if she should treasure it or throw it way. On the front was a picture of two young girls dancing and twirling, wraithlike in the bright light and long shadows, in that ethereal state just before the sun goes down.

The card in her thin-skinned hands shook as she contemplated the day she had last seen her sisters dancing. The wheel chair creaked from the tremor that now strained through her body. She hated the sound, the rhythm implying energy when all it meant was an uncontrolled fight against the ungainly movements of cerebral palsy.

At the roadside the girls had collected the mail and bread from the rusty drum with its front cut out. It was game of danger to put your hand past the serrated edges that lay in wait to scratch them as the victor stole the first taste of the loaf of fresh white bread, wrapped as it was in smooth brown paper. Evelyn was under orders not to reach in as her palsied movement might cause her to hurt herself, so she never won the prize of bread so fresh it became sugar on the tongue.

The special stage the girls performed on was off limits to Evelyn who couldn't leave her wheel chair without help. The tree was white-barked and smooth, scrawled with secret messages from fairies and woodland sprites – conveying a magical choreography to the performers. This stage was a long, thick branch that was waist high to the pair of pre-teens artists. It grew oddly from the trunk, almost parallel to the ground.

After practising movements on the grass until their confidence grew, her sisters became more daring and started to pose on the tree. Evelyn thought they looked beautiful. Overwhelming pride in their graceful moves negated the jealousy she felt.

Well, it should have. She told herself over and over. 'They

aren't hurting me, they aren't hurting me.' But they were of course, by their exclusion and showing off the agility required for the routines.

The younger girls made up songs, plays and adventures together. Evelyn watched and applauded soundlessly with hands whose palms couldn't touch together. She'd wave and cheer while inside resentment grew, gripping hard and making a gnarly knot in her chest like the exposed roots of the tree, binding her to the pain of rejection.

Yes, it's true. Evelyn was the one to tell their parents about her sisters dancing and their poses, slanting the story with enough suspicion that implied they were deliberately posing for passing traffic. Something she was now sure was untrue in her geriatric reflection. But it could have been true. The girls had put themselves at great risk if a driver with ill intent had stopped. Surely a temptation to passersby. So she had justified her actions, telling the story to their parents as her spite-blinded vision saw it.

All she achieved was further alienation from the girls. She'd set no good example. They didn't see her intervention as helpful or protective. They saw right through to the jealousy that motivated their older sister to dob them in.

It was Evelyn who learned the lesson in this sisterly exchange. Evelyn should have left them to their artistry and dancing adventure. She reconciled herself that would never be included in any of the games made up by her younger siblings.

That the tree was called the 'No-No Tree' ever after was a payback from the girls. They ran to get the mail from the 'No-No Tree.' They raced for the school bus at the 'No-No Tree.' They carried the bread home from the 'No-No Tree.'

It was the day before Evelyn's fourteenth birthday when she spoke to their parents. Sixty years ago today. She'd had no chance to break into the younger girls' well established relationship after her role in the drama of the 'No-No Tree.' They had been tight from the moment the youngest was born, preferring to play as free spirits and not with a girl who couldn't run or climb or hide behind the chook-pen in a game of hide and seek.

The card was from her older brother, the first she ever received from him. How odd he'd pick this one. He knew Evelyn had broken the game and brought heavy discipline and a lifelong ban of playing in the tree. Perhaps he'd guessed about the life-long guilt she carried for spoiling the game.

In those days he avoided playing with the girls. He was always making something in the shed – he had a fascination with making things and undoing the making of things. Even if it only had two parts he'd still want to undo them and put them back together.

He lived overseas now and hadn't been in contact with his sisters for many years. Evelyn sighed, she should have been the one to reach out to him.

Their little sisters had both died during the previous year. She missed them desperately. In her mind's eye they danced still. They were like jewels on the necklace their mother wore to church, as they spun and cavorted with abandon on the tree.

Maybe her brother thought he could bring the last two siblings together, as if by breaking the silence the healing could begin.

Evelyn held the card, opened it and read 'To my sister Evelyn, who dances in her dreams.'

Trace the shadows

Rina Robinson

The last tiny bead was finally in place. Rani had spent long hours on this one elephant toy and now it was almost complete. There was always so much work to do, for so little. She was glad that she was able to scrape a living for her son and herself. Her work was good. The toys and jewellery she made went for high prices to the tourists.

Rani had memories. Lovely memories of being cradled in strong brown arms. Of warm nights, of love and passion, of being wanted. There were memories of perfumed trees and flowers, of colourful butterflies, of parakeets sitting on a branch outside a bedroom window, gently suggesting that possibly it was time for them all to wake.

There were other memories too. The times when Mr Singh would arrive each week to collect the items her husband, Dahn had made; when the payment for last week's items would be handed over and the orders for the next week's work would be placed. Back then, Rani would wear her second-best cotton sari and all her jewellery. She would take tea to refresh the men, or maybe lemonade in the hot season.

Mr Singh had thought very highly of Dahn's skills as a wood carver, and promised much. So far this had only resulted in a roof over her head, but Rani guessed this would have to be enough.

Although a considerable amount of what the tourists paid went to Mr Singh the trader, Rani was grateful that she had managed to escape the fate of her sister. Moyna was married off at fourteen to an old man, an acquaintance of their father.

The child, Lal peeped around the doorway.

'Yes, soon,' Rani said, rising from the floor to go to the cooking pot where the curry was nearly ready.

Rani was now a widow. Dahn, whom she had run away from home to marry, had died of cholera a year after their son was born.

Her father said it was retribution for not obeying the custom of allowing parents to arrange suitable husbands for daughters. However, her mother suggested that Rani should move back in with them. They would try hard to find a man who would, with a little persuasion, and perhaps a few hens, take on an older woman of twenty-two years with a small child, although it would be difficult. They refused to help her join her sister in Australia. Her heart sank.

They pressed her to move back home with them. Rani had refused their offer saying that she did not think it would be necessary. She was earning quite well and could still look after them both in their old age when the time came.

Many a time when she looked at her growing child, Rani gave thanks that the custom of 'suttee' was no longer in acted by taking the wife's life when her husband died. Her great, great, great grandmother had been put to death in this way, leaving the children to fend for themselves.

At least Lal would always have his own mother by his side. She was grateful too, that Lal would receive an education. She dreamed of him growing up strong and independent, possibly to become a doctor or a scientist. How Dahn would have liked to see that.

She missed Dahn terribly. How they loved one another, enough to brave, not only her parents, but his also, who felt that Rani was not the right caste for their handsome son and his family.

Rani would take the child, Lal, to see his grandparents from time to time, and they would give him presents and make a big fuss of him. Sometimes they would present Rani with a new sari, along with lots of advice. Rani would listen to the advice, then take her child back home to her own humble dwelling. So many times had it been suggested that the good looks and strong physique came from their side of the family, but Rani felt this was to keep the memory of their only son alive, and she was sorrowful for them.

When Dahn had fallen ill Mr Singh made sure everything that could be done for him was done, and this had taken a load from Rani's shoulders. But it had not prevented the inevitable happening, and Dahn had died believing Mr Singh's promise to look after Rani and the child.

Rani continued to work at her craft and care for Lal. She went for water each day, holding her head high, and she would cook the rice as usual and pretend that she did not grieve her beloved.

The day came when Mr Singh, deciding that Rani had grieved long enough, took it upon himself to call on her formally. He was wearing his best shirt and trousers and had his hair and beard trimmed.

'You are being alone now for nearly twelve months. It is not good for you to be alone,' he said, his head moving from side to side in rhythm with his speech. 'I am here now for you to name the day when we shall be married.'

Rani was appalled.

There had never been a time when she had considered marriage to this man. She did not like his yellow teeth, or his slimy way of looking at her. To her, he was only the source of her income, meagre though it was.

Mr Singh went on, 'It will be a simple ceremony, we are not to be having many people present because you are a woman with a child. This is enough for us to be keeping the wedding quiet.'

'But...' Rani started, but Mr Singh was not listening.

'I will be getting you a new sari. This will be having gold trimmings. We will be having Mrs Das to arrange for the wedding guests. She will be knowing what they will eat. It will be coming expensive, but it is only what people will be expecting from a man in my position.'

Rani tried again. 'Mr Singh, I am sure you are meaning well, but I cannot be marrying you.'

'Not marry me!' Mr Singh exploded. 'What are you meaning? Why would you not be marrying me? It is a good offer. I can be giving you all that you are needing.'

'Yes, but, I am afraid I do not love you, Mr Singh.'

'What has love to be doing with this? I was promising Dahn I would be looking after you always, and that is what I am doing. I am living up to my promise.'

'Mr Singh...' Rani started again.

'Is it that you are being afraid?'

Mr Singh's voice was gentler now and he joined his hands together and bowed his head ever so slightly.

'I will look after your child as if he were being my own son. This is because I am having very great affection for your husband. You are able to be going on with your work. I will not be stopping you from doing this, even though a wife of mine should be above labour.'

His hands now had reached above his shoulders and were waving about. 'You will be allowed to work until you are producing another son. Then you shall be living properly, with a maid, as befits the wife of a man in my high position in the community.'

Eventually Rani was able to convince Mr Singh that she had no intention of marrying again, that she was quite happy with the present arrangement.

Mr Singh went away, not even beginning to understand that Rani had loved her husband too much to want to replace him with another, just to be cared for.

A few weeks later, Mr Singh told Rani to move out of her bungalow into a smaller dwelling. He said he needed the house for some relatives that were coming to stay, and that she could move back in when they left.

This one, on the outskirts of the town, was not much more than a hut, with no veranda or doors. The floor was earth and the roof leaked badly in the monsoon rains.

Gradually, Mr Singh stopped taking the jewellery and toys Rani made, telling her that trade was falling off.

Rani had no way of knowing if this was true, but she tried instead to find another outlet for her work. Unfortunately no tourists ever came to this side of the village.

The little house was beginning to feel like a prison, with no escape. She missed the delightful perfume of frangipani which had surrounded the previous building. There was no Bougainvillea to brighten her day, just huts that were too close together, and sad poor people squatting around on dirt roads.

She was now quite thin, most of their food being given to Lal who would soon be expected to go to school. She was reluctant to go to her parents, to tell them she had failed. The memory of her father's wrath was still very much in her mind. 'You should be listening to me. I am knowing what is best for you,' her father had cried, when Rani told him she had met a particular boy, and wanted to marry him.

But Rani and Dahn had not listened. One night they crept quietly away together to get married.

Her wedding jewellery, when she sold it, did not fetch much, but it kept she and Lal for a few more months.

The day when she decided to make one more elephant toy. It would be the most beautiful of all, suitable as an heirloom for Lal to give to his children when he married.

The beads were now all in place. The two tiny tusks made of forbidden ivory stood proudly above the trunk. This, a labour of love, was not intended to be sold, ever.

Rani had strained her eyes over this one beautiful thing and now she knew she would be unlikely to make another one.

A shadow filled the doorway.

Rani looked up. Mr Singh was standing there wearing his best shirt and trousers, and his hair and beard were oiled.

Camping Under The Bridge

Christina Batey

I sighed. 'Yes, Mum, I'll be fine.'

'Well, ring if you need me. I'll be here to pick you up tomorrow.'

I shut the car door. But I saw her mouth forming the words 'Bye' and 'I love you'.

I don't know how Tahni Sawtell got my mobile number. It had taken me a long while to believe that it really was me she was texting, and not a wrong number. She seemed really keen to make sure I was coming. It was kinda weird, but, we'd spent some time together doing a history assignment last week. Maybe she decided I was all right, even good enough to join her little clique.

The others were just beginning to pull up. Even their parents' cars were cool. We had a fairly new Mazda, but they all had meaty-sounding Holdens and Fords. They all looked as though they had a thorough detail five minutes ago.

We would be camping overnight under the bridge that was in the movie. The one Lincoln Lewis was in. OMG is he hot! As we made our way down to the sandy riverbank, I wondered if my feet were stepping anywhere near where his had been. That would be so cool. I found a spot and began unpacking my tent.

'Oh, Amy, is it okay if me and Tahni have our tents next to each other?'

'Uh, yeah. Sure,' I said. I moved further down.

'Sorry, Amy. Jessica bagsed that spot.'

'Oh. Okay.'

I hauled my stuff down the bank. This time I had a good look around me before I started unpacking the tent. It was pretty easy to assemble and I'd done it heaps of times.

'Need a hand there?'

Lincoln Lewis had nothing on Dean Trent. I tried to think about getting the tent set up properly and not about Dean's sandy hair and big, brown eyes. Then I realised he had actually spoken to *me*.

'Oh. Sorry, Dean. Um, yeah. Okay,' I stammered.

He smiled. His mouth was a masterpiece of dentistry, and his perfect lips deserved all the special care he surely took to make them that smooth. He bent over and started straightening out the tent poles, and I tried not to look at how his muscles rippled under that tight, white t-shirt.

I wasn't much help. I didn't want to watch him too much,

because I didn't know how they would get an ambulance down here if I passed out. When he did get to a point where he needed a hand, I wasn't paying attention.

'There ya go,' he said, flashing that Da Vinci smile.

'Thanks,' I think I mumbled.

The sun blazed and the sand was already starting to burn my feet. I'd better put on some sunscreen or I was going to be a lobster before six. All along the riverbank, lithe, golden bodies were revealed in designer-label swimsuits. With measured carelessness, long, silver-tipped blonde hair was organised into ponytails, smooth over the scalp on the first attempt, even without a brush. I looked down at my blue rashie mounding over white shorts and even whiter, flabby legs. I quickly wrapped a towel around it all.

'Coming in?' Dean asked, ripping off his t-shirt in front of me as though I wouldn't notice. 'Come on, the water's great.'

No longer feeling the blistering sand, I trotted down and shed my towel, getting as much water over my chubbiness as quickly as possible. I ducked my head under. That would take care of the silly, frizzy curls at the side of my head until my hair dried again.

The river filled with girls. I had a fleeting thought that it was kind of weird that Dean was the only guy here. It wasn't as though he was the only guy in their group – there were always heaps of guys hanging around. Either the girls had either been forbidden to go if their boyfriends came, or maybe the boys couldn't make it for some reason. Or Dean was about to have a happy time all to himself. That last thought made my stomach turn.

We swam until the sun began to lengthen the shadows of the bridge. All the girls seemed to just naturally command attention. All I seemed to do was take up space. The sun caressed and painted them a deeper gold, but it just slapped me until I went a horrid shade of red.

They were better and more graceful at anything they did, whether it was gathering firewood or flirting with Dean. And I knew that they would be able to eat as many of those chips as they liked, where even the crackling of the packet being opened would put kilos on me. Mum made me pack some sandwiches for dinner. I shoved them to the bottom of my bag and pulled out my stash of chips and blocks of chocolate to add to the mix going around.

Dean flopped down beside me. 'I'm starving,'

'I've got some sandwiches if you want,' I said.

'Oh, yeah. I'll be in that.'

He took the whole package and scoffed down the lot.

'I've got some cake my mum made, too.'

'Sounds good.'

Someone started handing around a bottle. I watched it stop with most of the girls and thought I might get lucky and it would be empty by the time it reached me. Dean took a swig and offered it to me.

'Oh, no thanks.'

'Go on. One sip won't hurt.'

It wasn't as though I'd never had alcohol before. I sneaked some of Dad's scotch one night. Even though it was an expensive single malt it burned all the way down. This wasn't scotch, though. This was ... sherry, I think. And this bottle of sherry had just touched Dean Trent's lips. It would be as close to Dean Trent's lips as I was ever going to get.

Dad always says, 'when opportunity knocks, let him in and offer him a cup of tea.' So I took a little swig. It wasn't that bad, actually. Much better than scotch.

It wasn't the campfire scene you see in movies. There wasn't anyone playing a guitar, and no one except me stared moodily into the fire. The gentle flickering glow on everyone's faces fought a losing battle against the white glare of i-phones as they answered message after message. Even with this many friends around them there were still more, desperate to be a part of their lives somehow.

I took another swallow.

'Having fun?' Dean asked me.

'Not really,' I heard myself say. What a stupid sad sack am I? The most gorgeous guy in the known universe was sitting next to me and making conversation – what kind of idiot is going to be a wet fish and complain I wasn't having a good time?

Me, that's what kind.

Dean slipped his phone into his back pocket. He had to press his shoulder to mine to do so. 'Well, I'll just have to fix that, then. Hey, Tahni, hand that over, will ya?'

Tahni passed the sherry and Dean offered it to me. I must've drowned in the river and gone to heaven, because Dean Trent appears to care whether I'm having a good time!

We shared the bottle for a while, until a hand reached out and took it from me. Dean was really nice. I'd always thought that he knew how good-looking he was and used it to his advantage. Now I realised he was just ... outgoing.

'Yeah, I s'pose,' he said, when I said this to him. 'There's still a lot of people who think I'm an arsehole, though.'

'No way! You're a great person.'

'Thanks,' he said. 'You're a great person, too.'

I beamed up at him and didn't care if he could see my feelings painted all over my face.

'Let's go for a walk,' he said, holding out his hand to me.

He let go as soon as we disappeared into the darkness, and my heart sank. But then, the strong, scented warm bath that was his body enveloped me; his arm around my waist, the rest of him as close as he could get to my side.

'Sorry I didn't do that earlier. It's just that some of the other girls get a bit jealous.'

'That's okay,' I said. And it was.

Then, the impossible happened. It started with warm fumbling in the darkness and body heat very close to my face. That mouth wasn't just nice to look at – it was very useful in other ways, too.

I thought a guy like Dean would want to push further, and as I kissed him I debated inwardly whether I would let him. Of course, my body argued that an opportunity presented itself, and I really should offer it a cup of tea. In the end, Dean made the decision for me. He was a perfect gentleman, not even going for a second kiss.

'That was awesome,' I breathed.

'Yeah. Let's go back, hey.'

When we got back to the fire, some of the girls looked at us and giggled amongst themselves.

'Well, I reckon it's time for me to crash,' Dean said.

The girls all agreed. Everyone began making their way over to their tents.

Except my tent wasn't there. My sleeping bag and my stuff was there, lying on the sand. I shone my torch around. Nothing nearby. Then I caught the shape of something among the darkness of the river. It was my tent, slowly succumbing to the water.

Muffled giggling erupted into laughter. Spinning around, the torch caught the same face on each of them, heard the same donkey braying laughter coming out of them. Did they know how much they looked like each other? Was that the secret to getting into their special club?

I put the torch into my bag, picked it and my sleeping bag up, and walked away.

'Hey, hey . . . what was your name again?' I heard Dean shout. 'Hey, don't be like that. We were just having a bit of fun!'

Fun.

It wasn't very cold, thankfully, but it was getting windy. I snuggled further down into my sleeping bag and stewed in anger and humiliation. Deep down, I had known from that very first text message asking me to come, that they had something in mind. And all that crap with Dean – what sort of a retard did they take me for?

I had the alarm set on my phone, but didn't need it. The first drops of rain woke me up. It was nearly six o'clock. I hoped they were all late sleepers.

The drumming of the rain didn't wake them, but I knew that it leaking through the holes I had pierced in their tents would, later rather than sooner, I hoped. I wanted nice, soggy, frizzy hair for all of them. I grabbed my stuff and hurried out of there. Good on Mum, she was early, as she always liked to be.

I wish I could have been there when they woke up. Maybe I should have been harder, but I just couldn't let thousands of dollars' worth of designer-label clothing just go gurgling to the bottom of the river to join my fifty-dollar tent. Instead, I arranged all their bags in a little group in an inlet. Easily seen and nicely saturated.

Tahni had stupidly left her iPhone in top of her bag. I didn't throw it in the river. I didn't even steal it. Though I have to admit that both of those things did cross my mind. But I did take some photos and sent them 'to all'. I sent a copy of her phone book to my phone, as well. It might come in handy, some day.

I know what I did was silly and lame and probably piss-weak. I'll still be laughed at and humiliated come Monday, and for many, many days after that. I know what I did to them will probably never get out. But just knowing that I did it will make things a bit easier to bear.

Dean didn't get any special treatment from me. I thought about it, I really did, but I decided against it at the last moment. He'll just have a wet bag and tent to drag home, just like the rest of them. But the first thing I'm doing when I get home is logging onto Facebook and posting to everyone I know that Dean Trent kissed me.

Notoriety Not by Choice

Neridah Kentwell

Sydney Town, 1st March 1788

James Freeman was pouring sweat. He swayed as he stood under the gallows tree with a rope around his neck, beside the ladder that he would soon have to climb and have kicked from under him. All because he'd been starving from doing as much work as three men since they'd arrived. His twenty-year-old heart pounded as he shook with the fear of impending pain and the unknown quantity of death. He didn't want to die!

Two nights earlier another convict, Thomas Barrett, had been bestowed the dubious honour to be the first to be hanged here. But the job had been botched and he'd continued to kick in agony for some time while they'd all had to watch. James dreaded being executed the same way, having to experience hell before he actually left this earth.

His partner in crime William Shearman, supposedly his chum, had said James had been the one to obtain the flour they were charged with stealing. James had declared he'd found it in the woods but no-one had believed him. He remembered how his mouth had salivated for the large pudding they'd planned to share once William had boiled it up in the big copper. Now he was too terrified to feel anything as normal as hunger.

Earlier, the battalion had marched them here under arms, to receive their punishments. Now the air suddenly resounded with the beat of the Red Coats' drum - making him jump. It was pounding out his final minutes, and made him feel ill.

Reverend Johnson came forward and stood beside them to read from the bible, entreating them to repent with each verse, but James did not hear a word as his short life swept through his mind. He just hoped he'd get to see his Ma and Da in the after-life, if there really was one.

'Stop!'

All noise halted and the crowd of convicts and guards looked around in surprise. Major Ross, head of the Royal Marines, strode over to them and spoke to some of the soldiers. A declaration was then read out.

It was a reprieve, but it had a condition that went with it. James thought for a moment then reluctantly accepted with a nod. He didn't have any real choice. Two marines removed James's halter. William had also had his sentence changed, to 300 lashes.

James later realized that he'd only been given respite because of his youth, strength and size - his ability for the tough jobs that were needed so desperately by the new colony. In fact it was his second release from a sentenced capital punishment, as the first one had sent him here. He was decidedly free but at what price? This young Freeman could never now be truly free again.

He was the first to have his pardon written in the Pardons Register for the colony of Australia. The requirement put on his acquittal was going to be hard to carry out. He was also to never leave the colony, even if one day he could afford to. By this time he had fortunately already served over half of his seven year sentence that had originally been pronounced as the death penalty at the English Hertfordshire Lent Assize; for stealing by highway robbery.

James was born the youngest of six, in around 1768. His parents were most likely the John Freeman and Susannah Tophill who married on 25th October 1756 at the St Mary's Parish Church of Rickmansworth in Hertfordshire. They appeared to be so poor they were unable to contribute to the church's funds when he'd been baptized, as was the usual custom. The family's survival then went further downhill after his father died when young Jim was only eighteen months old.

Rickmansworth was a small market town at that time. The period was particularly tough on the labouring class because of the industrial revolution; farming land was taken back and many country folk were enticed to the cities, resulting in a real decline in their quality of life wherever they lived.

The fact that James joined a gang of males older than himself can be more easily understood in hindsight. He may have been pressured into the acts of highway robbery he was charged with, accompanying his twenty one year old and thirty year old associates. Possibly not fully understanding the extent to which it was morally and unlawfully wrong, he may have thought he had no other way to keep in with his desperately needed friends or obtain extra money, as labouring earned so little then, if he was working at all. So it was a quest for survival from limited choices, and young people rarely imagine they'll get caught.

Held at the St Albans Gaol when first captured, James went on to other Hertfordshire prisons after his sentencing had been changed, his age then said to be only sixteen years. He was next conveyed to the *Ceres* hulk which lay off Woolwich, on the south bank of the River Thames in South East London. Finally he embarked on the *Alexander* with another 194 male convicts, for their banishment to the other side of the world. They sailed on board the largest transport ship of the First Fleet, mastered by Duncan Sinclair who was not known for his kindness. After an arduous trip and being sent straight out into hard labour on limited rations, James had not learnt his lesson yet.

As the first official hangman and common executioner in the colony, the first act he had been pardoned to carry out occurred on the 2nd May 1788, in between his other jobs toiling to set up the town. A John Bennett was the lucky recipient; lucky only because James did what was required of him in a quick and capable manner, just as Governor Phillip had hoped. During the rest of his official term, he finished the lives of fifteen souls in total, as 'finisher of the law'. These included six marines and a woman, Ann Davis. He did not find his occasional assignments easy by any means, as there is also a record of him becoming inebriated, abusive and out of his hut after hours, which put another black mark against his name.

With his sentence finally completed and the arrival of the Third Fleet in July 1791, James's life took a turn for the better. He met Mary Edwards, from the female convict ship *Mary Ann*, who had been sent out in the period when they were desperate for females. The crime of stealing shoes, which both Mary and her husband were accused of having taken together in England, resulted in only Mary being transported.

However, within fourteen months of Mary's arrival in August 1792, James became the father of baby Mary. In December two years later, Bethia was born.

Sadly James's lucky time didn't hold. Although Mary Edwards had been attracted and committed to him for some years, they never married and their relationship did not last. Perhaps it was because he didn't receive any land in the land of plenty. He'd broken the law twice during his colonial punishment and so paid the price by not being given a grant. Or maybe he became hard to live with as his mental state deteriorated from the deaths he'd had to carry out, a Post Traumatic Stress Disorder that was nowhere near to being understood in these early days, which may also have resulted in a drinking problem.

For whatever reason she left, Mary Edwards was then able to pick and choose with a 10:1 ratio of men to women, and by 1800 she'd had another daughter, Susannah, this time to Abraham Martin.

A further blow was to be dealt to James in the form of his eldest daughter's death on the 5th October 1801, aged just eight. The Freeman family name was placed firmly on her burial transcription, unlike her birth record which has both of their last names, giving the appearance that James was the one that had to carry out that hard business. There is no cause of death recorded so who can say if, or where, blame was laid between the parents?

James's other daughter Bethia, only 2 ⅓ years younger than her sister, felt her death cruelly too, as no doubt they would have been great play friends at that age. However, when Bethia grew up to have her own children, she named her first born female twin for her half-sister Susannah and the male one for her father James; it was her third born child who became Mary for her mother and sister.

James continued to work physically hard as a labourer, keeping his slate clean, and doesn't appear in any more documents until the NSW 1828 Census. He was then reported as James Thurman, aged 63 years, finally classed with an absolute pardon after so many years under the cloud of a conditional one. Following a lifetime of inadequate amounts of good food and oral hygiene, missing front teeth would no doubt have forced him to pronounce his own name incorrectly; this was then recorded literally by the clerk collecting the data.

Written under the employment column of the census, James was sadly listed as a pauper at that time. Living with a farmer at Richmond, Thomas Miles and his family, and after a lifetime of hard physical toil that caused his body to break down without the benefit of land and sons to take care of his old age, he was finally forced to live off others' charity.

His end came only four years later when, after passing away in Windsor Hospital, he was buried on the 28th January 1830 almost exactly forty two years after his arrival here. He was buried in an unmarked grave in the St. Matthews Anglican Church cemetery at Windsor, in the historic Hawkesbury River district.

James left behind the legacy of what can so easily result from poverty and a lack of emotional and family support. Although his Freeman surname was unable to be passed down, the fact that his only surviving daughter gave him ten grandchildren means his descendants are numerous. The family has overcome what was once the shameful secret of having a convict hangman as a relative, particularly so for many of the earlier generations, to a place where we can now celebrate James and his amazing story.

Don't think twice, it'll be Alright!

Mary Gabb

I was exposed to risky exploits from a very early age; an easily conscripted participant in the death-defying games invented by my brother, Ted. Deferring to his seniority, the first activity in which I was a less than willing player, involved a challenge to Providence; a test of courage; while simultaneously testing speed and agility.

At age six I had not much of either, and was even more disadvantaged at the time by severely painful ankles and knees. *Road runner* we called this game and Ted was in charge. We took turns running across the road in front of oncoming traffic.

You had to wait until the last possible moment before making the desperate dash. And the winner was the one who remained alive while allowing the smallest distance between himself and the approaching car. It was an exciting game and attracted neighbour kids like a magnet. The older ones had got the distance down to a terrifyingly small gap between themselves and their allotted vehicle.

'It'll be alright,' reassured Ted, the junior school steeplechase champion, when it was my turn. 'I'll go up the bank a bit and be your lookout so you have a bit more time. When I say go ... run! Don't think twice!'

I didn't see the next vehicle, but as I limped across the road, I felt its draught as it whipped behind me. With an angry screeching of brakes and tyres the truck stopped and a familiar figure, livid and furious, emerged from the grey Power Board Truck. There was no escape. Deliberately, the driver removed his belt. Punishment was immediate. Our father was not amused.

'It'll be alright,' my brother reassured as I climbed aboard the makeshift lift. My mother's broom was taking on a new life and purpose. Attached to each end was a length of bale-string, which after many frustrating attempts, was slung around the lowest branch of an ancient macrocarpa tree in our paddock.

I was supposed to ride the twelve foot distance on this device, unfazed. Ted and his friends had constructed a tree house and they were proud of their efforts. I was to be the first guest to inspect their precarious structure.

The boys had tomahawked toe holds into the dark gnarled bark of the tree, but my legs were too short to reach from toe hold to toe hold. Not to be thwarted, they had constructed a 'lift' for my benefit. It was their first practical experiment in pulleys. One boy on the end of each rope pulled, but it did not occur to them to try to synchronize their efforts.

While see-sawing precariously on the perilous ascent, I clung leech-like, and wondered whether the adventure was worth it. Their experience with friction however was limited, and about a foot away from the point where I might have found a hand hold, one of the abused ropes frayed and broke.

I was dumped unceremoniously onto the aromatic pine needles below, not too severely bruised but with my courage and faith somewhat dented. Against my better judgment, I made it on the second attempt with stronger ropes and more experienced operators. And triumphantly viewing the world from their eagle's eyrie, I silently prayed that the return trip would be alright.

'It'll be alright,' my brother confidently claimed as we stood on the banks of the swiftly flowing river half a mile from our house. I was eight years old and had just learned to dog paddle. 'If you get tired half way across, you can just lie on your back and rest; the current will pull you along,' said Ted. 'It is not quite as far as it looks. There's a sand bank about three quarters of the way across, you can stop there ... if you can touch the bottom,' he reassured. 'Look, I will stay beside you and give you a tow if you need it'.

Ignoring my futile objections and taking charge, he marched me up-river a chain or two trying to judge where the current might land us on the other side. With my brother's persistent urging I pushed off. He swam ahead.

'Come back!!' I screamed.

'You can do it,' he shouted over his shoulder.

Mid-river at the point of no return he turned and circled; I felt a push from behind. Exhausted, I rolled over on my back to rest awhile, but the banks of the river started to accelerate at an alarming pace. The significance of this did not escape me. I knew that just around the next bend, the river was sucked greedily into the dumping breakers of the Pacific Ocean. Terrified, I resumed dog-paddling with renewed energy. At last, burping and spluttering on dry ground on the other side, I was stranded and winded. But I basked in my brother's praise and was recharged.

'You did it!' Ted cheered.

He was right! It was alright.

'Just do it, it'll be alright,' my *tor*-mentor pleaded as he handed me the air-rifle. 'You can shoot me now, but don't tell Mum.' So saying, he wrapped himself tightly in an old eiderdown for protection. Chasing thieving birds from the two acre strawberry patch had become boring and tedious, and when I saw the air-rifle pointing at me with the command *'run'* I knew the challenge was real.

I tried to escape the line of fire but, frozen with fear, I couldn't move and I felt the sting of an air-gun pellet hit my left calf. Enraged, I didn't think twice but grimly accepted Ted's offer of retaliation and returned fire at point blank range. My bullet left a souvenir of our war, a hole in the eiderdown and in his shorts, as well as a pink patch on his bum. Thankfully, it was alright, and I felt avenged.

'Get in, it will be alright,' said Ted as he stuffed me into the rusted 40 gallon drum. 'Don't move! We're off!'

I heard this reassurance with skepticism from the dark innards of the drum. Leaping on top of the drum with a thud, at first he slowly walked backwards, then ran as the drum gathered momentum and bounced down the grassy hill in our paddock. Inside, I bumped, and scrambled while he danced on top.

If I survived, I vowed to be an observer rather than a participant in future activities with my brother. Like a cork, I popped out dazed on to the soft, clean, sweet smelling grass at the bottom of the hill. My clothes, eyes and mouth were full of dusty fragments of rust. The world spun drunkenly, but I was alright.

When I was thirteen, my chauffeur to weekly music lesson was Ted.

'Get in,' he ordered one day, opening the driver's side door for me. 'You're driving!'

Without disclosing any outward sign of reluctance, I got in—and drove, while Ted sat in the back seat giving the occasional instruction on gear changing while he read a comic. My hands on the steering wheel were slippery with perspiration. He did not know and I would never tell that I was terrified. I knew that in the 30 kilometre return trip a narrow bridge and a small township had to be negotiated. So I fixed my eyes on the left hand verge of the road, unable to look at the oncoming traffic. If I did, I knew I would be sucked irresistibly into its path.

'Mrs Waterhouse, do you love your children?' the local pastor quizzed my mother soon afterwards.

'Of course I do,' was her unsuspecting reply.

'Well I saw your daughter yesterday, driving through Awakeri at 70 kms per hour in a 40 kms per hour speed zone,' he announced.

'You must be mistaken,' she said. 'She doesn't drive.'

'Ask them,' he responded.

Music lessons were temporarily suspended. Mother now took charge and we were grounded. And the day I turned fifteen I had my driving license!

The Toy

Marilyn Linn

'Do you know what I've been thinking?' asked Geoff out of the blue, in the middle of the TV News.

'No. What?' I replied, only half listening.

'I reckon we ought to buy a four-wheel drive and do a long trip – Darwin and around the West,' he said, 'when we take our long service at the end of the year. What do you reckon?'

Well, it didn't really matter what I thought, and within the month we were the proud owners of a brand new Toyota 4x4 (four-wheel drive) nicknamed "The Toy".

We drove through the suburbs and shopping centres looking down on the lesser mortals of the world around us, from our perch on high. The Toy had five forward gears and power steering so the actual driving of it was quite easy. I learned how to haul myself into it. Being only five feet tall, the step was higher than my knees! I developed a modest 'slide and drop' routine to get out, being careful about the skirt not getting hitched up at the back.

'Oh, don't worry about the other gear lever. I'll teach you about that later, on the dirt.' Geoff knew all of this stuff. I don't know where he learned it. Not with me, that is for sure, and we had been married for nearly thirty years at the time.

Then the day of reckoning arrived. With a group of friends

who were experienced 4x4 devotees, we were off to learn about off-road driving. With enthusiasm (Geoff) and trepidation (me), we headed for the nearby forest, where access tracks were ideal for trying out tough cars and their super-cool drivers.

The hubs were locked in and detailed instructions were issued by our friends about the use of the other gear lever, speeds, and the rescue equipment if things turned sour. 'Just stay calm and let the car do its work. You'll be right. We've got the snatch-straps handy if you tip or get stuck,' they exclaimed, reassuringly.

It didn't take long for me to recognise that I hated 30° downhill gradients. The little tip-metre on the dashboard showed me we were in the extreme angle range. What goes down must come up, and when I could only see the brilliant blue sky and the treetops, or had to brace myself against slipping forwards or sideways, I was not having fun.

'Don't bite the seat belt, idiot,' yelled Geoff, my loving spouse. 'Open your eyes,' he urged. 'We won't tip.' His promise sounded hollow as we slid and slithered over loose rocky tracks. 'There is not much chance of us tipping over. We're going too slowly.' He tried to reassure me.

'But what if we get stuck at the bottom? There's no track here. Let me get out. I'll walk.'

'No you won't. You're being stupid. It's f u n. When we get on to a flatter track you can have a drive. Then you'll see.'

The promised flatter track was just over the crest of the rocky track and I hoped that we could now go home, but it was not to be.

'Come on. Have a go. Just go slowly and get the feel of it. You'll love it.'

I knew it meant a lot to Geoff for me to get the hang of this 4x4 driving and the track didn't look too bad. We had driven on worse looking stuff in the 'ordinary' car. So, with me reluctantly at the wheel, and under instruction from my husband, I put The Toy into the appropriate gear, and moved off.

We were on a rough track, but not too steep and progress was good. My heart was pounding and my palms were sweating. I can't say I was enjoying the experience much but I kept going. Then – THUD -. Some unexpected soft white sand grabbed the wheels and we almost came to a halt.

'Keep the revs up – keep going – don't let it stop – keep moving – keep moving – don't worry about the sliding from the back end…'

'Easy for you to say,' I yelled back.

'You're in Low Four. Keep going,' Geoff replied, a little irritably I thought. I was doing my best.

The Toy ploughed on. I didn't get stuck.

As soon as we reached a suitable spot, I stopped the car and refused to drive another inch that day.

I felt better after a cup of tea and a bit of a giggle.

The next weekend, off we went again. I even asked if I could have another drive.

'Of course you can. Today we're going to the hippo pits,' Geoff informed me, with a funny laugh. 'You'll love that.'

Well, I can tell you now that I didn't love that at all!
A pleasant forty-five-minute drive south through dairy-farm country and our convoy of 4WD's pulled into the yard of a farmhouse.

'Wait here. We won't be a mo'.'

The men, (the drivers,) went up to the house and the women were left sitting in the cars. A few minutes later, the blokes returned to their cars amid backslapping and guffawing. Geoff looked through the back window of our car and gave the thumbs-up to the others. The men waved to each other, mounted their thoroughbreds (read 4x4's), and off we went.

The dirt road rapidly deteriorated and the tyre tracks were filled with purplish-black muddy water. Progress slowed as we slid through the mud. Now I could see a huge expanse of water across the road but I could also see buildings. The buildings turned out to be milking sheds and the water was the hippo pit, the run-off from the washing out of the milking sheds. It covered about the area of the average house block.

The cowboys "circled the wagons" (stopped their cars) and again left the women in the cars while they approached and assessed the pungent black mud.

All aboard again and the process was explained to me. The most experienced driver, Jack, would go first, then we would follow and our son would bring up the rear. Once we were all through, we would change drivers and the girls could drive back through. Easy!

Hubs locked in, revs high, Car One set off. Two metres in and the nose of the car hit the black slop and it splashed up over the bonnet and front window. On the car ploughed. Waves of slush washing outwards as the wheel-deep mud allowed the car to pass.

Now it was our turn. My hands felt clammy and I would rather have been almost anywhere else but there.

Our trusty steed edged forward, revs building as we approached the pit. Geoff had his tongue poking out a bit and I'm sure that would have helped. Then a little more speed as we reached the edge and in we went, not exactly in the same place as Jack. As expected, the black mud slid over the front of the car, washing over the mud-guards disrespectfully. The back of the car danced mockingly around as the engine protested at the driver's expectations.

The front of our car dropped alarmingly. I screamed – said something rude, I think. The car stopped. Black mullock, half way up the sides, past the running board. Now what?

More bad language from me and some from Geoff.

'Okay. You get out and take the snatch strap with you. Jack will help you hook us up.'

'Why do I have to get out? Look at the mud! You must be mad! Anyway, the strap is too heavy for me. You get out.'

'Well, I can't get out. I have to drive.'

I sat there stubbornly.

Jack tried to save the situation by wading a little way towards us, up to his ankles, then he yelled, 'Throw the end of the snatch strap here.'

This turned out to be impossible and after much protest from me, I had to get out into thigh deep, cold, black, cow-poo mud. Jack retreated to dry ground.

'Hook the strap on the back before you get too far,' came the instructions.

I'd been drilled in the procedure for attaching the snatch strap before we left home. How did they know we would need it?

I made my way precariously through the bog, fearing that I would fall face first into it. The fear kept me upright. I gave Jack the heavy roll of snatch strap, dutifully and securely attached to the rear of our car, and made my way to higher, drier land and watched as Jack, Geoff and Mark, our son, extricated our car from the hippo pit.

Our son supervised. The snatch strap acts like a rubber band. An end is attached to each car and the one not stuck drives forward, or backwards in this case, until the strap is taut. This has the effect of yanking the stuck vehicle forward, or backwards, violently. The heroes had to repeat the process twice on this occasion.

The blokes tried to make a joke of the situation but I was in no mood to be jolly. I was wet, cold, muddy and smelly. The other women were quietly sitting in their warm dry cars, watching, sniggering.

With our car rescued, and all men very pleased with their efforts, our son decided he wanted to prove his manhood and have a go at the pit. He succeeded where we had failed. By now I was not speaking to anyone and Geoff decided that it would be best to take me home, still covered in drying "bovine business".

As the muck dried, little pieces fell off of my track pants and shoes onto the floor and seat of the car. I didn't care. I refused to take them off until I was home. I was uncomfortable and unhappy, sullen and non-communicative.

I never got my turn to play in the hippo pit but we had many more adventures in The Toy.

Some were fun, in retrospect, although I am still the butt of jokes about the hippo pit.

Country Snobs

Linda Brooks

The small, timber school with its dull grey asphalt playground was a typical Australian country school. The playing fields beyond the quadrangle were generous grassy areas, fenced by barbed wire to separate us from the cows that lived in the nearby paddocks. Those of us who hadn't travelled far, and that was most of us, didn't know any other way of life. All schools must be like ours.

Occasionally we had students who had come from The Mission

Field. We gathered around these new people with glee, bombarding them with questions about 'foreign places'. We found them universally reluctant to share their past lives with us. After we'd nagged them, we received a few unintelligible, mumbled phrases. Any further pestering ended in the Mission children telling us they wanted to forget all about wherever they'd been. We were a bunch of 'sticky beaks' and should leave them alone. We decided The Mission Field must have been akin to Prison of War camps—such was their angst at our questions.

Later of course, much later, we realised they just wanted to fit in and be like us. Our constant calling attention to their previous lives only made them feel as if they would never fit in. We locals had known each other all our lives and had no concept of 'fitting in' other than a strong desire not to be picked last for rounders, not to cry in front of the others and woe upon woes—never wet our pants. Some things could be lived down, but not that. If anyone suffered that dreadful fate, they had our undying sympathy, but in social terms—they might as well emigrate.

I knew nothing of aborigines, their customs or heritage. It was a long time before I stumbled on that most basic fact that 'they were here first'. Because my older brother claimed all television viewing rights due to seniority I'd watched many Westerns so I had an idea about American Indians, and immediately transposed their history to our indigenous people. I was enchanted by the lives of the 'redskins' and their culture and once spent an entire hot, slow Sunday begging Mum to change my name to Pocahontas because 'Linda' was boring.

With that background it was only natural that I desired to embrace my aboriginal compatriots. Or I would have, but I didn't lay eyes on a single one until I was 14 and in high school. Sadly, my new prospective aboriginal friend didn't like the look of me.

There was no embracing to be had with the only aborigine of my acquaintance. I must have seemed like an over-exuberant puppy and scared the poor kid.

Anything we saw on television was American and gave us very little idea of our own country beyond our small town experience.

We thought ourselves privileged indeed to have Dora Creek. It didn't occur to us to hold the dirty old Dora in disdain. After all, she was all we had—only movie stars had swimming pools. If we came out of the water looking like woolly mammoths because the marmite detritus stuck to our fine body hair, we didn't complain.

Our school swimming 'experiences' also took place in the muddy Dora, not far from 'the swing bridge'. I use the word 'experiences', because no-one actually taught us to swim. This was a source of great anxiety for me. On our family holidays I'd been able to fake the whole swimming process, just managing an awkward dog-paddle. However, here at the creek where the teachers would assess our swimming skills, it was a whole new ball game. One where humiliation was my only possible destination. I prayed for a sudden onset of smallpox.

Our teacher, Mr Solomon, lined us up on one side of the creek and was going to watch us swim across. Except that in my case he was going to watch me drown. The first half a dozen to arrive at the other side would be chosen to compete in The Swimming Carnival.

'We're going to compete with Strathfield High School this year,' boomed Mr Solomon.

'Oh great! City snobs,' I moaned.

'Keep that up Brooks, and you'll be sent back to school,' he threatened. Oh the joy—escape was possible. I only had to up the ante, give my teacher a bit more attitude and I'd be sent back to school. No-one would ever know my dark little secret.

'Well, *they are snobs*, Mr Solomon. When they came here for our last Sports Day all they did was look down their noses at us. Isn't that the definition of 'snob' Mr Solomon? Isn't it?'

I silently prayed for release, the long walk back to school, a thousand years detention—anything but the revelation I'd spent years playing in water without making significant progress through it. And *never* able to acquit myself at 'freestyle', faked or not, which was a crucial requirement.

'Be quiet and line up in the water with the others, Brooks.'

'But sir! Don't I get sent back to school?'

'No.'

'But you said!'

'Line up!'

My doom was sealed. The water was too deep to fake a crossing. I looked for a log. Perhaps I could hide behind it and sneak away. The other kids were squealing with excitement, thrilled at the thought of being chosen. I felt sick to my stomach. I was going to sink like a stone.

Solomon blew the whistle. The muddy waters of the creek foamed with the thrashing arms of dozens of kids. There were screams of delight as Solomon officially announced the winners who had earned the marvellous honour of representing the school. Cheers filled the air.

'Alright you lot! Swim back here and collect your gear.'

I didn't move. I scarcely dared to breathe. I couldn't believe Solomon hadn't noticed that I was still near him—on the wrong side of the creek, having never left. The kids were so excited, noisily splashing their way back, that for the first time in my school days, I escaped detection.

After arriving at the original side the kids began to scramble out and grab their clothes and towels. Solomon looked down at me with a quizzical expression.

'Brooks, get a move on! Get out of the water! We haven't got all day!'

'Yes sir!' I crowed, dizzy with relief.

The day of The Carnival came. We pretended not to see the shiny city bus. Our mouths were open with shock when the children stepped down from the bus adorned with hats and gloves. We looked down at our scruffy shoes, laces askew.

They lined up in perfect straight lines. We remembered being called 'higgledy-piggledy brown's cows' and shuddered. A few of the pristine Strathfield girls whispered and giggled quietly.

'Silence please!' said an elegant teacher as she inspected the lines of children. Our eyes popped. Their 'noise' would have been considered good behaviour to our teachers. We had an inkling why we were often called a 'rowdy lot'. One teacher had even declared he'd met heathens with better manners.

My excited question of 'Ooh, where did you meet heathens?' landed me outside for the rest of the class.

Our city counterparts eyed us as one would a group of feral animals shortly to be put down at the local vet's. This would not do at all! We girls huddled together. We had to defend ourselves against these distant, superior invaders. We devised cunning replies and prepared cutting barbs.

We needn't have bothered. None of them deigned to speak to us.

I Will Run When Summer Comes

Pauline Young

Summer! People in the hospital were talking about what a hot day it was outside. It was only late spring, but already the mercury was climbing.

A group of us sat in a circle in the therapy room of Cambridge Psychiatric Hospital, poring over our writings. Colleen, the nurse in charge waited patiently while we struggled with our problems on paper. The air was electric with the sound of rustling paper, scratching biros and the sighs of the patients. I hunched over my note pad, pen poised.

They say that summer is knocking at the door, and I will run when summer comes, I wrote.

After a very nasty episode when I thought I was dead, I now realized I was still alive, and that it was November, 1978. That I wasn't in some underground cavern of hell where the wallpaper pattern peeled off the walls to invade one's mind, or where you had no body, but drifted through the air uncoordinated, with nowhere to go and no-one to relate to.

Yes! I was alive at the age of thirty-six. Perhaps there were many more years to go before death – the real death, overtook me. Summer, and Christmas were mine after all. I must recover from my nervous mental illness and run, run, run!

Beatrice Fed the Ducks on Monday

Victoria Norton

Beatrice Ellington fed the ducks on Monday. Not with bread torn from a loaf gone stale – she knew that would clog their tiny stomachs and pollute the water. Instead, she tossed them salad greens that she picked from her garden on the edge of town.

She was fiercely defensive of her garden. All things lived in a complicated bio-network of unruliness. She no longer planted or weeded and would joyfully rub her hands together if a new seedling poked its head above the untilled soil. She loved that the free growing plants attracted little creatures.

To practise her post-stroke speech in the privacy of her own home, she carefully enunciated as she spoke aloud. Like a child drilled in a spelling bee she pronounced the botanical names of things she recognised. She spoke with care, setting her face in a fixed position, so the drooping muscles that spoiled the symmetry of her face wouldn't be so obvious.

'Eastern water dragon lizard – *Physignathus lesueurii*; Millipede – *Ommatoiulus moreleti*; Strawberry – *Rosaceae Frugaria*.'

Beatrice sometimes collected wild growing dandelions and milk thistles on her gait-challenged walk to the creek. On a rare day she would fling the ducks a half-cup of tangled red composting worms from the dank bin that sat near her rusted out rainwater tank.

As usual, the raucous ducks peddled across the creek to greet her, and like contestants in a dodgem car rally, they caromed off each other and onto the water's edge. She had not named the birds, yet she recognised each one by the pattern on their faces, their rank within the group and she knew their family histories. She particularly liked a small bird with a damaged wing, an edge dweller somewhat ostracised from the group. She felt empathy within her own damaged body.

On this Monday, she threw grub-eaten spinach and gone-to-seed lettuce as far as she could into the water with her palsied left arm. She called her condition the 'Accident' to distance herself from owning it, this awful thing that stole so much from her.

She was rueful in the knowledge that trying to selectively feed the natives she nicknamed her Blackies, had no effect on the proliferation and distribution of the non-indigenous Muscovys and Mallards. Yet she was perversely persistent. One time she hurled a rock into the creek to frighten away the interlopers, but the swoosh and ripple made the Blackies fly off too, and for a time she lost their trust.

She disliked the aggressive Mallards, which out-bred the natives after a few breeding seasons because they weren't fussy who they mated with. At times she felt like being more proactive, that perhaps she would join a wild life group like WIRES, but she knew she'd never put herself out there like that. She was never comfortable with people and had always been scornful of petty social machinations. Since the Accident she distanced herself from human contact as much as she could.

On this particular Monday, at just past sun-up, Beatrice set up camp. She picked this bend in the creek because it was a place the joggers and mothers-with-prams avoided, due to the rocky path. She settled on the only seat at this part of the water's edge, a solid concrete bench.

First she placed the linen tea towel on the seat beside her. It was the same one she used for her dishes last night, but it wasn't really dirty. The dishes were clean weren't they?

Next she unpacked the open wicker basket. Beatrice rubbed the handle, so smooth and shiny to her touch, and remembered her mother filling it with fragrant, fresh cut roses from the garden. A single rose bush, a Mr Lincoln, clung to a broken lattice frame and was all that remained of the dozens of prize-winning roses her mother had cultivated. The thorny bush tore at Beatrice's tissue-thin skin, as frail as heirloom wedding veil, so she didn't cut the flowers anymore, she simply watched them bloom and die.

Her mother inexplicably left the family home the day after Beatrice's sixteenth birthday, and was not heard from again. Beatrice remembered her with anger and sorrow. A ritual with a single red petal, plucked from the Lincoln and wiped gently across her cheek, mimicked the lost touch of her mother's hand. This memory brought on sudden tears that she caught in her hands. Childlike, she wiped them against the sleeves of her dress. It wouldn't do to show her emotions. Her father had insisted long ago that she keep her feelings in check, now a habit hard to break.

She poured herself tea and opened the greaseproof paper that wrapped her wholemeal toast.

Finally, she unclipped the little jar of strawberry jam, the last one she preserved before the Accident attacked and stole her cooking dexterity.

The Lions Club had installed the seat in memory of some community hero who died there trying to save a child from drowning. She was there when it happened, but right now she couldn't recall his name, or the child's. He went on to become Mayor. She turned to read the name on the little brass plaque on the back of the chair, trying to take it in as a new memory, but knowing she never would.

In her agitation she dropped the knife. It left a smear of red across her dress and she wiped off as much as she could. Wash day was on Wednesday, and she'd wear the frock till then.

The local hooligans had defaced the seat with paint-sprayed uncouth words and illegible scribbles. This annoyed her less than to share the spot on the water's edge with anyone else. Especially that Harold Whitaker, cantankerous old man that he was. He had a horrible barking dog, a terrier of some sort, and it always chased her Blackies away.

Here he was now – ready to interfere with her day. He'd stop and talk to her. He'd want to weed her garden. Paint her fence. Fix her guttering. Sometimes he'd say her home was going to wrack and ruin. Other times he'd go on about how she fed the ducks, that it upset nature's balance and encouraged vermin. Why did he not see she was doing exactly the opposite of all that? It was her determined choice to let the weeds, flowers, vegetables, garden creatures and ducks flourish – survivors all, just as she was.

She turned her body sharply to indicate her irritation and the ratty brim of her straw hat tipped to shade her damaged face. She had stopped speaking to him after last year's illness. He had no need to know how much she struggled to speak at all, or how much her once fine features had changed.

On this day he strode on past her with determined boot steps. He seemed in a hurry. He didn't have the dog with him. He didn't even glance her way. Perhaps he was looking for his dog.

'How rude,' she muttered.

Something niggled in her memory; a deep male voice; the scent of orange blossom; a vague picture of a strong, chiselled face; the sensual touch of a hand held tenderly; the taste of desire in a kiss. But it didn't coalesce into anything meaningful. She promptly forgot about Harold as her thoughts rambled on.

The day passed. Her evening began as she poured a small glass of sweet sherry at eight o'clock. She looked forward to reading, a favourite pursuit since girlhood.

She laid her current selection of library books out in a fan shape around the table, herself the pivot point. Who afforded new books these days? Piles of overdue books with pages marked with coloured papers towered negligently on the floor and on the other chairs. She must return them soon or they would suspend her borrowing privileges again. Her planning and organising was corrupted by the damage to her mind, making her irritable, a feeling more and more common to her.

She sat in her dining room under the dusty Tiffany lamp until the carriage clock on the mantle chimed midnight to conclude her work.

She scrimped on her budget to leave room for stationery supplies, which she ordered by mail and paid for by cheque. A tall bearded man delivered them in his white van. Beatrice thought he was a sticky beak, always asking how she was when it was none of his business.

For many years Beatrice had written a commentary on every book or novel she read, fiction and non-fiction, and posted it addressed to the author in care of the publisher.

Now, on this Monday, working to complete her evening's work, she tidied away the papers and pens. Beatrice wrote her letters by hand, in the beautiful, flourishing cursive script she was taught by the nuns of Saint Joseph's. She thought of her many years' service to the Parish typing letters for Father O'Reilly and receiving a small stipend in return. She couldn't cope after the Accident and Father reluctantly let her go. That she was able to write at all was a Blessing.

She was working her way through several large and beautifully illustrated books. Today's tome was 'Every Australian Bird Illustrated.' Editors allowed so many mistakes to go through to publication, there were commas missing and don't get her started on the dashes!

One letter she received very plainly said she was not welcome to comment. She simply corrected the spelling and added a comma and sent it back without a stamp.

Infrequently, an editor's reply to her unsolicited corrections and critiques would thank her for her comments, and this spurred her on. She was sure that her correction of incomplete facts and distorted knowledge was helping future readers to a better definition or a better resource. She expected the publishers to rely on her exemplary effort, and reprint each corrected work, although she never checked. It would have been good to mention whether she had a career.

Her peeve of the moment was the Mynah bird, brought here from India to combat insects in the cane fields, a hundred and fifty years ago. Invaders like the feral ducks, they took up places in nature occupied by the little natives, like the yellow-eyed miners and the honeyeaters.

Beatrice contemplated poisoning all the feral birds. She read a Bryce Courtenay novel that told of a man who wrapped bread around snail bait pellets, and fed them strategically to pigeons, a last meal of sorts. But the thought of causing pain to any of God's creatures stopped her. They were doing what came naturally to them after all. They were in the wrong place and the wrong time for reasons of human choice, not their own. So she fretted over them, angry and sympathetic at the same time.

She didn't waste her time with magazines or newspapers, and never owned a television. The single social medium she allowed herself was the 1930's Astor Bakelite radio inherited from her father. He had set it on the ABC radio frequency and she saw no need to change it. Its crackly voice kept her company.

She had used the public telephone at the end of her street twice in her life. When she called an ambulance to her father after his heart attack and seven years later to call the doctor on the night he died. She hadn't needed to make a call since then.

She bathed with a flannel and a bar of yellow Sunlight soap in a chipped enamel bowl of warm water, filled by a kettle heated on the gas stove. She refused to pay for hot water and she switched her system off after her father's funeral.

The night Beatrice suffered the stroke was as ordinary as any other, until it was time to pack away her books. Stunned, she fell and hit her forehead on the chair. Thinking the fall was the cause of the excruciating pain in her head, she took herself to bed, guiltily foregoing her bathing routine. Next morning, as she tried to leave her bed, she realised something was terribly wrong with her left arm and leg. Stoically, as was her nature, she struggled against the semi-paralysis, and for the last time, drove her father's old Holden to the doctor in town.

Beatrice made ready for bed now, in an iron-framed single that had always been in her room. She wouldn't use her father's larger room, or double bed. She felt uncomfortable in there. It was a parental place, off limits as a child. But there had been no choice about nursing him so intimately in that room, after his heart attack had left him bedridden. She gave the room a thorough clean after he died, stripped the bed, and locked the door with a click of finality.

Beatrice listened to the familiar creaky sounds of her own bed, a soothing creak that had long been a lullaby. Her crooked body lay still and ready for sleep, cradled by the kapok in her musty mattress.

Her thoughts stirred in reminiscence. There came an idea of feeling loved and cherished, and somehow Harold's handsome young face came to mind. She imagined his strong arms around her and met the look of longing in his eyes.

A proposal of marriage; a delicious kiss; then the refusal she had to give – it was her duty to care for her father.

Was it a fantasy? Her recollection was not to be trusted.

She reached under her pillow, inside the cover, the one her mother decorated with embroidered violets, now threadbare but oh so smooth on a tired face. She withdrew a small blue velvet bag and took out a ring. Heavy gold told of its age, the ruby warm and glowing even in the darkened room. She put it to her lips, savouring the memory, and then gently replaced it under her pillow.

Beatrice fed the ducks on Tuesday.

Black and White

Linda Visman

The stockman reaches down from his horse and catches the fleeing woman's sun-bleached hair. He pulls back hard, jerking her off her feet. She screams. Her coolamon flies into the air then crashes onto the rocks next to the creek bed. The berries she'd been collecting scatter across the ground. As the woman falls back, arms whirling, he lets her go and jumps off his horse. She twists her almost naked body, trying to regain her balance, but lands awkwardly. There is a sharp crack and her leg collapses under her. The man ignores the sound, dragging his trousers down as he falls upon her. She struggles, but is hindered by her broken leg. He is quick.

He stands over her, buttoning up his trousers. He speaks and, though she understands no word of what he says, the woman hears the scorn in his voice. The strange language of the white man means nothing to her. She lies still and tense, waiting for him to leave so she can crawl away. But he does not go. Instead, he reaches down and picks up a large rock. He speaks again, and this time his voice seems to express regret. As he raises the rock above his head, the woman's eyes widen and she jerks away, a last, futile lunge. The young girl, hiding among the bushes gasps through the fingers jammed into her mouth. Although she wants to look away, she cannot. The rock descends, finding its mark with a hollow, sickening thud. The man mounts his horse and rides off along the dry, sandy creekbed. He doesn't look back, but the girl waits until he is out of sight before she runs to where her mother lies, unmoving.

Connie was short and slender, her wrinkled face and black eyes lively and alert. She couldn't walk as far or as fast as she had seventy years ago, but she still wandered down to the little community store to collect her pension and to buy her bread and meat. She walked slowly but confidently, feeling the warmth of the red dirt on her brown, calloused feet, her faithful dogs trailing along behind her. Now and then she greeted those she passed. Most, if not all of the people in this community were her relatives. Many were her direct descendants. She couldn't count them – she'd never learned about numbers and writing or how to manage them like some of her kids and grandkids could. She could hardly even speak any English; just a few words, like 'good' and 'yes' and 'store'. But Connie knew every adult and every child and their skin relationship to everyone else in the community.

The old woman had seen all but one of her generation – and too many of those younger than her - depart for the spirit world. She'd participated in *Sorry Business* for four of her five children, several grandchildren and even some great-grandchildren. Sometimes she felt lonely, wondering why she'd remained active to such an advanced age when so many had succumbed to the perils of the new world - grog and disease, violence and fast cars. She'd always been healthy. The only reason she'd gone to the Clinic that first time thirty years ago was so they could sew up a bad cut on her leg. She'd been a few times since, or the sisters had visited her at home. But that was just to have regular check-ups to keep the clinic mob happy.

Connie didn't know how old she was. The Clinic sister had to guess her age when she first registered with them. They told her she had to have a birth date - everyone did - for the records. They thought then that she was about sixty years old, so they allocated her the first of January 1916. It didn't really mean anything to her, but having a birth date made it easier for the Clinic, so she went along with it. However she wasn't going to tell any of those sisters now about the pain that sometimes stabbed her in the chest, making her weak and dizzy and needing to rest for a while. She wanted to die in her own country, not far, far away in a white man's hospital. These whitefellas sure had funny ideas.

As she arrived at the store, Patsy joined her. Connie's granddaughter always tried to be with her when she went shopping – especially on pension day, which it was today. Patsy had been to school and knew about money. She made sure the storekeeper or his assistant didn't overcharge her grandmother and that she received the proper change. She also helped carry Connie's groceries back to the *Women's Camp* – a house in the community where they both lived.

Connie had gone to the *Women's Camp* when her husband died, way back when it was just a humpy in the bush, separated from the main camp to keep them apart from the men. She chuckled as the memory came to her. It had been good to have peace. That was before they'd been granted this bit of land, and before any houses - tin sheds at first - were built. Lots of women had spent time in the *Women's Camp* since then. Now, just a couple of old women, two younger widows and their kids, and several young, unmarried women and girls lived in the house with her. The old women relied on the younger ones to do the heavier jobs, to sort out problems with Welfare, or to nurse them when they were sick. The older women minded the kids and passed on the old stories, trying to keep them alive.

It was good to know there was someone to care for her if she needed it. It reminded her of when she'd been a child and of her mother's tenderness. Sometimes, Connie let her mind drift back to her childhood. Back to the good times she'd had with her clan as they moved about the bush in search of food; sometimes feeding well, and at other times going without for days at a time. She'd had a different name then, one that only a few of the older members of the clan remembered now. Most people used the name *Connie* when they were talking with whitefellas. Otherwise they referred to her as 'old woman' or 'grandmother' or by her relationship to a particular person.

Patsy helped her to pull out the heavy kangaroo tail from the big shop freezer. It was nowhere near as good as the kangaroos the men got, but it was better than going without. The men who still went out hunting used guns and four-wheel-drives now instead of going on foot with spears. It was too easy. Connie found some steak in the freezer too. She gave it to Patsy to carry and went to the shelves to get the packets of dried soup mix and noodles she'd add to it to make a stew. Some of the women at the *Women's Camp* didn't get their pension this week, so she had to buy enough for them as well. When they got their money next week, they'd help feed her – that's if they didn't gamble it away first or have to give it to their kids or grandkids.

More thoughts of long ago came to her as she watched a mother giving in to her child's noisy demand for cool-drink and potato chips. Life had been so much harder when she was young. There'd been no luxuries, but they'd had fun. Until that day, that is. The day she'd been out looking for berries with her mother, collecting the delicious fruit in a wooden coolamon. When the memory of that day came, she always tried to put it aside. Those days were gone now, and it was no good dwelling on the evil things that had been done to the women and girls of both her clan and others. She didn't feel bitterness to other white men over it – only a few bad ones had done those things - but she would never forget it.

Her mother's sister had taken over the care of Connie and her siblings. Connie had grown up and married a man of the right *skin* and given birth to their five children. They lived on the cattle station, supplementing their rations of beef, sugar, tea and flour with bush tucker, but still carrying out traditional ceremonies. Her husband was a stockman, and her life was very different to that of her mother, but she'd been content with it.

She was worried for the younger ones now. There were many of them, but the past thirty years had gradually distanced her people even more from their traditional ways. Change had come as they got easier access to town - and to sit-down money. Now they didn't have to work for what they needed, and they always wanted more than they had. Fast, noisy cars and television, grog and violence had come to their peaceful, isolated community. Young people didn't want to work. They didn't want to go to school. They didn't have that old respect for their elders any more. The *Law* was being watered down and corrupted. How would they fare if they were taken back in time to live the old ways? Connie sighed and shook her head.

She stood now at the counter with her small pile of purchases. As she waited for the shopkeeper to ring up the items on his cash register, she peered through the front door into the dusty glare of another hot, dry afternoon. Her eyes no longer saw clearly, but she could hear and just make out several young men skylarking noisily in front of the store. Maybe some of her grandsons.

Last night, several men had come back to the community from town, and brought grog with them. Connie had found it hard to sleep as they shouted and argued and sang, and roared around in their cars all night. Only as the sun came up had things quietened down. These disruptions to their formerly quiet life had become a frequent occurrence. The community was supposed to be dry – no grog, but there was nobody to enforce the law. A couple of the elders themselves were drunk, and the police only came when there was actual violence. It took a couple of hours to drive from their station in a far community, and usually they had too many other things to cope with.

Patsy checked Connie's change and gave it to her. Connie put the notes inside her bra; neither of them owned a purse, and gave the coins back to Patsy - she'd only lose them. Her granddaughter picked up the bags of groceries and went through the door ahead of her. Immediately they came outside onto the concrete area in front of the store, they were surrounded by a chattering group of young men and boys. Most of them were her grandsons and great-grandsons, and the older ones had spent their welfare money, a lot of it on grog. A couple still found it hard to walk straight after their night on the booze.

'I got no money for smoke.'

'Old lady, you give me money for cool-drink.'

Even those too young to get sit-down money demanded their share.

'I got nothing. You gimme money for ice cream.'

No matter how hard she tried, Patsy couldn't protect Connie from this *humbugging*. The old way of sharing whatever was available - the meat, the witchetty grubs, the bush bananas, the berries - had come down to this. Young men, who had never proven themselves deserving of it, now standing over an old woman to take what little she had for herself. Connie reached inside her dress and pulled out the money Patsy had given her. Patiently, one note at a time, she handed over the remains of her fortnightly pension cheque. A thought came to her, not for the first time - the Old Ones would be ashamed of their descendants.

But Connie at least had her groceries, and all those in the Women's Camp would eat well tonight.

'Flying Doctor plane come get you tomorrow, Connie. Take you to hospital. They look after you there. Give you medicine for pain.'

Connie smiled and shook her head at Patsy's translated words. The pale, sombre-faced doctor meant well, but he just didn't know her way. She gazed across the yard as they made their plans for her care. From her iron-framed bed on the packed red sand outside the Women's house, she could see most of the community - the houses and clinic, the school and store. Those conveniences had been meant to help her people but had, instead, shackled them to the fringes of an alien way of life.

Now it was time to carry out her own plan.

She makes her way slowly along the creek bed, stumbling at times. The last few miles across country have been difficult and painful. Her granddaughter had dropped her off where the bush track ran out and, reluctantly, driven off. After that the old woman struggled on alone, resting often, her weakened body tiring rapidly. A straggly bush catches her eye. She stops to pick a few of the black berries and her toothless gums chew them with pleasure, remembering. She is tired, and the familiar pain stabs with an unaccustomed intensity. She sits slowly and carefully on the sand and leans back against a smooth, sun-warmed rock. Her eyes close and soon, her raspy, shallow breathing eases. The tangy taste of berries lingers on her tongue. The pain fades, then departs completely.

She opens her eyes to see someone walking towards her. A figure she knows well, naked but for a hair belt and carrying a coolamon. Wild, sun-streaked hair forms a halo about her head.

The newcomer smiles at the old woman and speaks her true name.

'Why are you sleeping when we have many berries to gather? Come on Daughter. Don't be so lazy.'

The old woman jumps up and runs across the sand, amazed at how freely and painlessly she moves. She slips her hand into her mother's. Then, as they wander along the banks of the creek, gathering their black berries, the young girl runs and skips and calls excitedly to her mother. A light echo of her voice rises, then evaporates among the surrounding trees and rocks.

The sun sets on the still form of an old woman, lying on the sandy creek bed.

Author's note: This story is fictional. However it is based on real people, places and events that happened as late as the 1930s and 1940s in Central Australia, and on conditions that still exist in many remote indigenous communities today.

Becoming Country Bumpkins

Julie Cochrane

We sat in silence and gloomily peered through the misty windows of our family car at the main street of Adelong. It had taken us several long hours to make the arduous 284 mile trip along the Hume Highway from Sydney. We were tired, not to mention just a little irritable, and we were finding it very difficult to share in Dad's excitement about our new hometown.

The cold winter rain pelted down on the sedan roof and windows and added to the bleak mood that had begun to permeate the car interior.

'Is this *it*?' my sister asked in a grim voice - just *slightly* tinged with hope that Dad might say something like, 'No! Of course not! We're just stopping here for a break...'

Sadly, my father's response was one that we were all dreading.

'Yes, this is it!'

I couldn't believe it.

When Dad and Mum had first announced to us four kids that Dad had bought his own accountancy business 'in the country' and that we would be leaving Sydney, I wasn't sure what to think about it. It was 1964 and I was 12 years old. The thought of leaving my home, Grandparents, my church and school friends ... all that was familiar to me, was a little daunting.

Even so, there was alongside the fear of the unknown, a rather 'grown-up' sense of adventure that presented itself. Dad had softened the blow about leaving Sydney by explaining that living 'in the country' would be like living at Auntie Doll and Uncle Jack's place. Aunty Doll and Uncle Jack lived on a dairy farm on the NSW South Coast, and we kids had wonderful memories of visits filled with fun and laughter trying to milk the cows at the dairy, being chased by cranky bulls in the paddock, hiding in the hay sheds, tractor rides, and great country cooking...mmm, what kid *wouldn't* want to live in the country! Dad also pointed out that we would be able to own bikes in the country – because it was a lot safer to ride them there than in the city. *Yes!* I'd always wanted a 2-wheeler bike!

A couple of weeks later Mum and Dad took us 'in to town' to David Jones to buy some new clothes for our future new life in the country. Because we were going to live in the Snowy Mountains, we needed to stock up on winter woollies. I chose a tan and black hounds-tooth pinafore and coat, some tartan tights and 'sensible' shoes. These shopping outings in the centre of Sydney were rare for us as a family, so this added to the importance of the new direction our lives were about to take.

But on this *first* day of our 'new life in the country', this first miserably grey and wet day parked in the main street of Adelong, all thoughts of adventure seem to evaporate. Looking out through the relentless pounding of raindrops at the old wooden buildings, together with ancient gnarled and naked trees (spattered with starling droppings) that lined the main street, it was hard to feel optimistic about our new life!

Dad had parked the car outside an old building that looked as though it was about to fall over. The word *Accountant* was painted across the glass front door and Dad told us this was his 'new' office.

Silence.

We all got out and looked over the new office.

Mmmm...

After we got back into the car, we each suddenly found our voices and began passionately expressing our change of heart about moving to the country! Poor Dad – looking back now he must have been a bit discouraged himself – but there was no way he was letting on to us. We drove another 12 miles to Tumut where we stayed the night in a motel. Tumut was a much bigger, more 'civilised' town. I'm not sure how it happened, but somewhere in the night a decision was reached that the family would live in Tumut, not Adelong, and that Dad would drive the 12 miles to work each day (thanks Mum!).

And so it was.

For the next 13 years my family lived a country life in Tumut and my Dad drove the 12 miles to Adelong each day, six days a week, to The Office. I lived with them until I left school and moved to Teachers' College in Wagga Wagga, a large city with a population of 60,000 or so, around 65 miles away from home.

In the early days of my country life there were some adjustments to be made.

Entering my teen years in the country did have some definite drawbacks. The all-important fashion stakes for one. The Tumut Co-Op had little to offer a contemporary teen, but fortunately for my sister and I our family made regular trips back to Sydney to visit our grandparents, and this occasionally meant purchasing some new clothes as well. My country friends would be green with envy on my return when I announced that I had bought whatever I was wearing in *Sydney*!

This was also my first experience in attending a co-ed school. *And* having a male teacher!

It was all a little odd at first, but once I fell in love with Christopher Simpson, everything seemed to fall into place.

I admit to feeling a certain amount of pride at having come from the *Big City* and this was reinforced by the subtle admiration of my new-found friends. At first I deliberately resisted the Country Bumpkin ways of my new world, although secretly enjoying the warmth and openness of country folk. There was a freedom and easiness of life there that even as an 12 year old I was conscious of and appreciated.

Dad bought a lovely block of land in Tumut, high on a hill overlooking the town and eventually built a very contemporary and unusual home for us there. Mum's brother was an architect and so had volunteered to design it. The house was the talk of the town for many years.

Dad made friends with the Adelong community – most of whom had become his clients. Many of these clients were 'on the land' - graziers and farmers – and occasionally we would visit them on their properties. I remember loving the rides on tractors, or in the back of the jeeps, as the farmer would proudly (and bumpily) show us around his property. After the tour we'd arrive back at the farmhouse and get stuck into the lavish afternoon tea set out on the table. Huge scones with jam and cream, pikelets, sponge cakes and the like laid out of the best family china plates. Dad has always been interested in yarns about the past and he would encourage these men to share their stories of life on the land. I loved listening in. Many times Dad would come home from The Office with a 'beast' – a sheep or calf – that a farmer had slaughtered and cut up, to give to Dad in lieu of paying for tax work. The beast filled our freezer and kept us in meat for months. These country people were so generous and friendly.

The simplicity of country life fostered a community spirit that isn't easily found in the city. Family lives continually interacted in a variety of ways. For example, my friend Judy's parents owned the Fruit Shop, Libby's parents owned the local Jewellers store, Elizabeth's parents owned the local cinema (once, on Elizabeth's 16th birthday, her Dad let us all into the cinema to watch a private viewing of the latest James Bond movie!), and our (unpaid) church minister owned the local Pharmacy.

Dad was friends with the police officer in Adelong, that made it easy for me when I turned sixteen years and nine months, to get my driver's licence through him, rather than to go through one of the Driving Schools. When we were building our house, Dad's contacts in the local building trade helped with cost price articles. AND because he knew the owner of Adelong Produce Store, we had *free* (used) plastic fertiliser bags to use in lieu of toboggans when we went to Kiandra's snowfields on weekends!

Yes, it didn't take me too long to accept the Country Bumpkin way of life.

Listening Behind the Door

Louise Elizabeth

Mum always said that you never hear good about yourself if you listen at doors. I put this advice to the back of my mind, as I eased open the door to the conference room. I didn't expect to hear anything about me, but rather I wanted to know what my conniving husband was planning for the company.

I should have listened to mum.

The low-life was going to bestow on me the guilt for his embezzlement. He had accessed my desk and left incriminating evidence. To add insult to injury, he wanted to hire a hit-man to rid him of that 'pesky bitch'. I had to control my urge to walk in and let him know what I thought of him, but I remembered the pre-nuptial I had signed. I tip-toed away, searched my desk, and found the details of the Swiss bank account. *Really this is so passé.* I stood in the general office and my eyes searched for a likely recipient. That red-head, Sally, he spent so much time teaching, although I doubt it has anything to do with our printing business, she would do. Her door was open and I nonchalantly walked in and slipped the document in the back of her velvet-covered notebook. I was just about to check the contents when I heard footsteps.

By the time he came into the room, I was picking up

documents from the photocopier.

'Hello, dear. Everything okay?'

'Yes, of course.' He pecked me on the cheek.

'Good. I'm meeting Zoe for lunch, back by 2.30.'

'Okay. Enjoy.' He smiled insincerely. 'Sorry I can't come.' He looked back at the conference room. 'Too much to do.'

'Don't work too hard.'

As I walked out, I saw he already had his mobile out, ready to make a call.

It was a real pity he was standing so close to the stairwell, when Sally was frogmarched by the police towards the lift. She managed to kick him in the family jewels. He fell back, lost his balance, and thumped down the stairs. Such a pity.

I wonder how long I'll have to wear black. Luckily, the proceeds of the key-man policy, enabled me to have made a whole range of outfits suitable for a grieving widow.

I am Autumn

Christina Batey

When an autumn leaf falls from the tree, it seems such a silent and delicate thing, the way it gently sways and flitters, carried on gentle currents of air as it dances its way to the ground. But I imagine there would be a thousand sounds of agony up close.

A screeching tear as cell rips from cell, stem divorced from bark, and the leaf falls, howling through space, shoved and buffeted by tiny winds as it struggles downward. I wonder if birds and insects can hear that. Do they take the sounds of Armageddon all around them as their cue to take cover and prepare for the long months of hardship ahead?

I should have listened to that leaf as it fell.

I watched the tiny, golden dance of destruction, and played with Cameron's shirt in my hand. I don't know how I noticed such an insignificant mark hiding among the stripes. It could be anything; pen ink, a blotch from a bubble jet printer, or a particularly nasty clump of train grime. But I looked at it, and the first thing that popped into my mind was mascara; a tiny smudge, watered away to nothing where the black stripe turned to white.

I sipped my coffee and watched more agony fall in a golden shower from the tree, shielded from the cacophony by my ineffective human ears and the kitchen window.

Cameron breezed into the kitchen, flicking on the kettle and popping bread into the toaster, taking a slight detour in his travels to plant a kiss on my cheek. 'Morning, Darling.'

'Cameron, what's this?' I held the shirt out for his inspection.

He squinted at it. 'That? I don't know, a pen or something.'

The morning fog cleared and I hung the shirt on the line. It was pristine again, tugging against the pegs and playing in the breeze like a child.

I had hoped that this would be the end of it; that all my doubts and suspicions of the morning would be washed away with the tiny stain. But the thoughts were ground-in, and it would take more than a normal cycle to wash them away.

There had been tension lately. A distance I couldn't name had set in. As though he had been away on a long journey full of exotic adventures, and while he had expanded in mind, I had stayed home, expanding my mind with piles of dirty dishes and extended hours at the office.

Perhaps that is how it is. Cameron, always a shy computer-nerd, had found a job where his skills were not just appreciated, but celebrated, and his self-confidence grew as his clientele grew larger and more important. His company's latest contract had made the biggest change. The months he'd been working on it changed his walk, his dress, his manner of speaking.

I had always been proud of the man inside, but now that inner man was emerging. Others noticed it, too.

My friends kept asking, 'What happened to Cameron? Has he had a nip and tuck? He's gorgeous!'

I laughed and nodded. I was so proud. And so guilt-ridden about the jealousy I felt – he was spreading his wings and taking flight, and I was grounded, frozen, as though in hibernation.

'Delicious dinner, Honey,' Cameron said, as he dug in. We were enjoying something that lately had become rare: a dinner together.

'Thanks,' I replied.

He looked up at me and smiled. For a moment, all the black thoughts disappeared. Across the table sat a man who loved me, and it showed in that smile, one he hadn't shown me for months.

'So, how was work today?' I asked him.

'Oh, great. We're finally getting somewhere on that French account. Oh, that reminds me. You're coming to a conference on Friday night.'

I pulled a face, knowing I looked fifteen as I did it. 'But they're so boring.'

'I know. But I need you there hanging on my arm and looking stunning, as you always do.'

The only good thing about schmoozing Cameron's boring clients was the preparation. I could go out and get my hair done, have a facial, a mani-pedi, and buy a whole new outfit.

I met Julia and Denise for coffee the next day.

'I saw a dress today,' I said. 'I love it, but I just don't know if it loves me.'

The girls grinned at each other. 'You know us, trophy wife,' said Julia, 'we take great pleasure in telling you when your arse looks big in something!'

We finished our coffee and headed for the boutique. The girls 'oohed' and 'aahed' over the dress as I took it from the rack.

'Yes, I know it's gorgeous,' I said, 'but all that can change once I put it on. So be very, *very* honest.' I slipped into the dressing cubicle.

'So, how is Cameron?' Denise called through the curtain. 'I haven't seen him in ages.'

'I know. He's had this big project he's been working on,' I said.

'It looks as though it's about to all go through, so I can start seeing a bit more of him, soon.'

'Not to mention how much fun you're going to have 'catching up', if you know what I mean!'

I pulled back the curtain. 'You can say that again. It's been very quiet in that department. And we can get back to trying for a baby.'

There was a pause from the other side of the curtain. I knew the girls were looking at each other with *that* look. But I didn't care what the doctors said.

I pulled back the curtain. 'Well, what do you think?'

'I think it's amazing on you,' Julia said.

'Me too,' said Denise.

Where was my favourite lipstick? It wasn't in my cosmetics bag. Then I remembered I had worn it at the last 'girls' night out' and slipped it straight into the pocket of my jeans. When I had staggered home, I left it on the kitchen window sill. Don't ask me why. I clicked out to the kitchen and retrieved the lipstick. From the window I could see a liquid amber tree in the distance in her autumn dress, afire with crimson, russet and terracotta. A beautiful, vibrant dance before she sleeps for winter.

'You look gorgeous, Hon,' said Cameron.

He looked not too bad himself – crisp, young and alive. He and the tree were two brilliant objects in the grey landscape framed by the window. He smiled tightly, a bundle of nerves.

I rubbed his shoulder. 'Don't worry, you'll be fine,' I said.

Cameron's excuses continued, yet the account with the large company had been secured. The long hours to get the systems set-up and running were over. He stood before me as I accused him.

His shoulders drooped. He sighed and something I could

almost call relief settled on his face. 'Her name is Katie.'

'Katie.' I turned, staring into the combustion fire, trying to let it sink in. I wanted to be one of those logs, flames curling around me, gently licking, consuming. A warm, comforting way to be destroyed. My heart was frozen. Tiny shards of ice were breaking off with every laboured beat.

'She's pregnant. I'm the father.'

More shards shattered away and did their work on my head and behind my eyes. The next heartbeat melted them a little, giving me room to think for a moment.

'What is she going to do about it?' I asked.

'She is going to keep it. *We're* going to keep it.'

The splinters gathered together in a solid mass, and I couldn't move.

'Katie and I are so happy. I've never been so happy in my life.'

They were words that should have filled me with warmth and sunshine. They were cotton-wool words that wormed their way down my throat to choke me.

'We want...'

'Get out.'

I stood up and walked away to stand and gaze out of the kitchen window. Outside, the last tiny golden leaf detached from the tree and made its descent. I heard the front door close.

Now I am Winter.

The Gold Statue

Mary Gabb

She was hurrying through Adelaide Rundle mall, her backpack loaded with books and papers, when her shoe caught in a paving stone. She stumbled, scattering her load in every direction, and landed inelegantly at the feet of a gold statue. 'Damn,' she muttered under her breath, gingerly flexing her ankle to see if it was sprained. *Great, nothing damaged*, she thought.

She struggled to her feet awkwardly and chased flying papers before they were trampled and spoiled by the busy pedestrian traffic. She did not want to be late for her tutorial—she needed help with a difficult assignment. At this time of day people were intent on their own business. Not a soul stopped to help her.

'You could be a bit helpful,' she muttered to the statue. It was gold all over; a gold emotionless face, gold hat, jacket, vest, shirt and trousers, gold gloves and gold shoes. A stray wisp of russet gold hair escaping from his top hat was the only clue to another identity. He irritated her. A useless symbol of decadence she thought in this day of so much social deprivation. Surely he could have chosen some other artistic form for his busking. Reloading her backpack with the vagrant papers and books, she directed a surreptitious kick at the shins of the gold statue. There was no reaction or response. Its pose and expression were inflexible as though carved in pure gold. She wondered why anyone would spend his life doing something so useless and unproductive.

'No brain, no heart,' she hissed. Then, with her load once more intact, and cheeks flushed with annoyance she sped on her way to her tutorial.

Even though it was not the shortest route to class, she deliberately detoured by the gold statue the following day. A gold bandage was tied around the right leg of the annoying figure. She blushed. His posture seemed to have changed very slightly, and she thought his cupped hand was extended. It seemed to be directed towards her. She swerved away, noticing a subtle change in the expression of the face of the statue. Was it real or was it her imagination? Momentarily, she thought she saw a disappointed expression flash across his face. *Dumb stupid thing to do*, she thought, *standing there for hours when he could be doing something useful.* But she had to concede that standing there for hours on end in the same pose day after day would take a bit of stamina and quite a bit of courage.

Was it curiosity caused her to pass by the statue again the next day on her way to class? When she saw him next his leg was still bandaged and she thought she detected a small wink from the motionless figure. *Dork!* she thought. She averted her gaze, giving the statue a wide berth and marched on without a sideways glance.

The busker's spot was empty when she next passed by on her way home. *Some people have nice working hours,* she thought, *wonder if he's got a real job.* She felt vaguely disappointed at his absence.

Again she deliberately left home ten minutes earlier the next morning, to see if the bandage was still there. It was, and again the statue's fixed pose seemed changed in a subtle way. Today his cupped hand was definitely pointing towards her. *What does he think he is doing?* she puzzled. Feeling guilty she hurried on. Throughout the day and all that evening curiosity was eating her. She slept uneasily, and in the morning she felt foolish that the image of the gold statue had invaded her mind, and was haunting her.

The extended hand—again distinctly directed towards her the next day, taunted her. Curiosity got the better of her. An irresistible force beyond her control dragged her closer. Glancing sideways into the cupped hand she saw it relax and slightly open as she approached. In the outstretched hand lay three jelly beans. The statue's expression remained inscrutable and fixed. She quickly transferred the jelly beans into her own hand, and without acknowledgement quickened her pace. Out of sight she wrapped the jelly beans in a tissue, carefully put them in her pocked, and hurried off to her class. Her blue eyes danced and sparkled. She was preoccupied all day, finding it difficult to concentrate. Classes dragged and the day seemed to be endless.

The statue was not there on her way home. She was disappointed.

The next morning she once more left home earlier than she needed—to keep another silent rendezvous with her mute statue. He was in the same place, with the same fixed expressionless face.

'Here,' she said, 'have these back. I only eat red ones.'

She deposited the three jelly beans into his outstretched hand. She thought she saw a shadow cross the statue's face, and the eyes seemed to darken as she turned away. She grinned to herself and hurried on her way without a backward glance.

She thought she noticed a look of triumph on the face of the statue at her next encounter. His extended hand unmistakably followed her. Reducing her pace and moving closer, she looked into the gold face and caught a gleam in his eyes and a widening of the pupils. She inspected his hand. In it were three red jelly beans. She took them, popped one in her mouth, and flashed a dazzling smile at the still expressionless statue. As she hurried on her way, her blue eyes shone with satisfaction.

A silver haired lady with blue twinkling eyes hugged her six year-old granddaughter sitting on her knee. In her hand was a framed photo of a young couple. The young man with russet gold hair, was dressed formally but wearing ridiculous gold shoes. He looked animated and proud. The bride was dressed in a shimmering gown of gold satin.

'Tell me the story again, Grandma,' begged the child, 'about you and the golden statue!'

Keeping an eye on things

Rina Robinson

'I wish she'd gone to Greenleaf Retirement Village up the road,' said Mrs Shirley Wilmot as she poured herself another cup of tea.

Mrs Wilmot, unlike the other two carers with whom she shared morning tea today, was the full-time senior carer in the hostel of the 'Rose Arbour' complex. They had been talking about Hilda, the newest arrival.

'She's not that bad, I find her rather amusing really,' part-timer Sally Maine said.

'Oh, you can afford to be generous. You're not the one cleaning up after her,' Shirley retorted.

Hilda had arrived at 'Rose Arbour' only two weeks ago but she'd already made her presence felt. She really kept the staff on their toes. So much so, that they began to feel worn out 'keeping an eye on' her.

It wasn't so much what Hilda said as what she did.

The first day she scattered her stuff all over the shared bedroom she'd been allocated. Not only her own things which she'd refused to put into the drawers, but she had also thrown out the other resident's clothing from her drawers.

It was unfortunate that Mary Smith had been in sick bay for a week when Hilda came to share the room. The staff had tried to tidy up, but without much success. Poor, neat Mary got a nasty shock when she found she had to share temporarily. She was not one to complain, so she kept quiet. But now her clothes were not arranged in order. Not only that but she couldn't find her knickers anywhere.

Then there was the incident of "the letters". It was usual for staff to put incoming mail in a pile on the desk before sorting them out after breakfast. Hilda got there first. Her method of sorting them was to tear in half those envelopes with names she didn't recognise. She didn't know many of the other residents, so by the time staff arrived, nearly all the envelopes had been ripped in two.

'Tell Sally about last Wednesday,' Shirley Wilmott suggested.

'About the pot plants, you mean?' Robyn smiled. 'Yes, well, I was in with Matron getting the rosters. Suddenly we heard an almighty crash. We rushed out to see Hilda standing by the small table in the hall. You know, where we keep several pot plants?'

Sally nodded.

Robyn went on, 'One of the larger pots was on the floor,

smashed. There was soil everywhere. Not only that, Hilda had turned the two smaller ones upside down. You can imagine the mess.'

'What was she trying to do?' Sally asked.

Robyn imitated Hilda. ' "They're weeds, all weeds!" She'd got it into her head that the Peperonias must be weeds because they don't have flowers. So she'd thrown them out.'

'What happened?'

'Matron took Hilda to the dining room while I got the dustpan and brush. After I'd cleaned up the mess Matron told me to find a job for Hilda. You know, kind of keep her occupied for the morning. It's not as if Hilda is incapable, or frail, it's just that she seems to be, well, destructive.'

'You can say that again!' Mrs Wilmott laughed.

'I thought I was doing the right thing. I thought the woman might be keen on gardening. So I gave her a few of the new pots and suggested she plant some of those daffodil bulbs that came last week.'

'Seems like a good idea.' Sally laughed.

'Yes, I thought so.' Robyn went on. 'Simple. I didn't think anybody could get that wrong. But when I saw the result I had to smile. You'll never guess what she did. She put the bulb mix in all right. There they were, lined up, twelve small pots, each with a little plant tag sticking up! No bulbs, just the tags, planted neatly. The bulbs were still in the box they came in.'

The three women burst out laughing.

'Hilda really is something else, isn't she? Come on. We'd better get a move on.'

They washed up the tea things and went about their duties.

Thursday was the usual day for visiting volunteer entertainment groups. This week it was a small choir who called themselves the 'Symphonics'.

After breakfast the residents gathered in the lounge ready for their usual exercise session. When later the volunteers arrived, the residents were pleased to sit in the easy chairs and wait patiently. Hilda went into the reception area. The choir formed to stand next to the small organ. The Symphonics leader said how happy they were to be here again, and announced the first half of the programme. Before she'd finished her announcement she started to sneeze and couldn't stop. Mrs Wilmott picked up the flowers and returned them to where they belonged. Then she made sure that Hilda was sitting down again.

The pianist started to play. The choir sang, 'The Skye Boat song', a tenor sang 'Danny Boy' and this was followed by a medley of Lloyd Webber's songs. The next item was announced. It would be 'The Nun's Chorus'. Mrs Wilmott, there to 'keep an eye on things', pursed her lips. A bit ambitious, she thought.

Hilda got out of her chair, walked across to the choir and stood beside the sopranos. A few singers fidgeted and looked uneasy. Shirley Wilmott thought she'd better move Hilda away. But then she decided that Hilda couldn't do any harm just standing there. The organ began softly. The beautiful waltz melody gradually increased in volume. Then one voice rose above the others. All heads turned towards Hilda. The usual solo soprano, a pleasant lady, just let Hilda sing on. Hilda was in her element. She was transported to another world and happily sang with the others until the program ended.

The next Saturday, visitor's day, Shirley Wilmott handed around the little cakes at afternoon tea. She paused for a moment beside Matron who was talking to Hilda's niece. 'Pleased to see you again, Miss Bergman,' Matron said.

Kylie Bergman said, 'How is Aunt Hilda settling in?'

Matron said, 'We know very little of Hilda's early history. She does not talk much. But she sang with the visiting choir the other day. It was lovely.'

Kylie smiled. 'Oh, I know. She doesn't talk because she believes she has to save her voice. In her younger days she sang in opera.'

'Oh really, I didn't know that. Was she famous?'

'I have quite a few glamour photos. And some of when she did some modelling.'

'Ah! That would explain a lot.'

'Do you have problems with her then?'

'Oh no! But she needs something to keep her occupied, I think.' Matron was silent for a moment. Then she said, 'I might have the perfect solution. Do you think Hilda would like to start a small choir here at Rose Arbour?'

'I think she'd love to do that!'

Matron was so pleased with herself she beamed. 'Mrs Wilmott here will get her started, won't you Shirley? You know what to do.'

Shirley was not at all sure how she would go about getting Hilda started on this new project. But it was her job to 'keep an eye on things'. She knew she would have to find a way.

That night she had a dream. She was singing in a choir but suddenly lost her voice. She croaked along as best she could but... suddenly she sat up in bed in a lather of sweat. As soon as she got to the retirement home she went to find Hilda. 'Hilda, will you find a few ladies who can sing, please.' Hilda gave Shirley an odd look, but she went away, and brought back three ladies.

Shirley said to the first one, 'I believe you sing, would you like to sing for me?' The woman beamed and started to sing 'Love letters in the sand'. Others joined in and very soon another woman came and joined in. Then another came. Soon they were all happily singing unaccompanied. Shirley stood beside Hilda.

'What do you think, Hilda? Will they win a competition, do you think?'

'Oh no, not like that, they won't. Would you like me to lick them into shape?'

'Oh, would you? Shall I get Maud Pearce, the organist?'

Hilda drew herself up, 'If you would be so kind, my dear.'

Six months later, the 'Rose Arbour' choir were winning competitions against much younger teams of singers. And no more pot plants were overturned.

Preparing for Surgery

Marilyn Linn

One evening after Brianna had gone to bed, Max and Pam were sharing a quiet moment when Pam began crying.

'Whatever's the matter Pammy?' He leaned closer and placed his arm around her shoulders.

'I'm worried,' she sobbed, 'You know I have an appointment to see the paediatric plastics specialist on Tuesday, with Brianna, and we all know what it's about. I feel so guilty. How could I have let that happen to our gorgeous baby girl?'

'I'm coming with you, you know that, too. I've made

arrangements for the day off. Don't fret about it. Nobody blames you. It was an accident.' Max closed his eyes. He knew Pam would keep talking. He'd heard it all before.

'Yes, it was an accident, but many people think I should've been more careful. One uppity trainee doctor said he thought I caused it so I could get more attention for myself. Munchausen by Proxy, he called it. You know what that is. He blamed me, straight out. Oh Max! If only we could take back the moment.'

'We can't change it, Pam. We have to deal with it and we have to let Brianna have her say about the treatment, too. She's ten now and quite a smart little cookie. Perhaps we can have a few alternative plans, or ideas sorted out in our minds. Then we can talk about it with her tomorrow afternoon. Do you still have the list of things Dr Richards gave us a few years ago?'

'I have, somewhere,' Pam responded between small shallow sobs. 'I'll look for it tomorrow … no … I'll do it right now.' Pam stood quickly and hurried into the small office where they kept all their paperwork.

In moments she returned to the settee and gave Max the papers and a small booklet she had been keeping safe for two years.

'All we really have to decide is if we are ready to go ahead with surgery. If we think Brianna is ready. Let's set time aside after dinner on Sunday and we'll talk about it all. We'll call it a family conference and Brianna will know it's important.'

'What choices do we have, Max?'

Max flicked over a few pages and started reading out some of the things Dr Richards had mentioned. 'There's skin grafting. That's the one I'm most worried about,' said Max.

'Then there is the toe separation, and the ear repair and the cheek repair. Those last two both require skin grafts. I can't see anything here about separating her underarm from her torso though. This might be a big one. I think we'll have to wait until we see the doctor, don't you?'

Pam nodded silently. She leaned into Max and read the pages as he turned them. There was nothing new. They had read it before and talked about it before.

'I think I'll take Dolly out for a last chance toilet stop, and then go to bed,' said Pam, rising reluctantly from the settee. Pam took the half-grown puppy outside and was gone for several minutes.

Max decided to go and check on progress. He saw Pam sitting on the grass. 'What are you two doing?' he asked.

'Well, Dolly's peed and I'm sitting here watching her run around the garden. So much energy, and it's bed-time,' said Pam. She held out her hand and Max helped her up off the damp grass. Dolly noticed them moving and came bouncing over. Pam scooped her up into her arms. 'You're a dear little dog and I'm glad we've got you.'

Earlier in the day, Pam had told Brianna they needed to have a short chat about seeing the doctor, soon. Brianna had shrugged nonchalantly and gone on with her drawing.

Sunday evening soon came and after dinner the planned family conference was about to begin.

When the family of three were sitting around the conference table, Brianna announced, 'I know what it's about. It's about me having surgery. I know I have to. I wish I knew what needs doing the most.'

'Do you have anything in particular you would like done first?' asked Pam.

'Nothing, nothing at all, *ever*, would be my choice,' said Brianna.

'That may be an option to mention to your doctor on Tuesday,' said Max.

'I have thought about it,' said Brianna, after a long pause. 'There are things I'd like to be able to do and if the surgery could help with those things, perhaps ...' she stopped.

'Could we make a short list, do you think?' said Pam.

'I have reasons for what I'd prefer done, Mum, things I'd like to do, but I don't want a list. No list.'

Pam persisted. 'Do you have a list of questions you want to ask Dr Richards, then?'

'I'll write myself a short list of words tomorrow, like key words we learn about at school.'

'You learn about key words, do you? Is that in English class?'

'No. It's actually in computer. You have to learn to look for key words so you don't have to read every single word. We are learning to do it in the Library too, to make it easier and quicker to find stuff on a page you need, for research, for example. But you can't read a novel like that or you'll miss half the story.'

'Really?' Pam didn't know what else to say.

'Can you give us a clue what you want to ask the doctor about, Brianna?' Max wanted to stay on track with the discussion.

'Not right now. No. Sorry Dad. I'll let you know something tomorrow after dinner.' Brianna folded her arms indicating she had finished.

'Okay. Let's call this meeting adjourned until after dinner tomorrow, Monday night.' Max stood up and pushed his chair into the table. 'Come on, Pam. Meeting over.'

After dinner was finished on Monday night and the tabled cleared, Max reminded Brianna of the meeting. 'You have time to get ready for bed first. Off you go.'

'Really Dad? Do I have to?' Brianna scowled at her father.

'Have you made a list of some sort?' Max asked.

Brianna stomped off to her room and came back in her pyjamas, with her school bag. 'It's in here, but I don't want to read it to you. Some of it is private.'

'Please read one of the things you want to talk to the doctor about,' Max said, as they settled around the table again.

Brianna fiddled and scratched around in her bag and eventually produced a crumpled piece of paper.

'I want to ask about my foot.' Brianna began in a rush. 'I want to get my toes separated so I can wear ordinary shoes and sandals, instead of these clompy runners that don't run. Marcie at school taught us the Health Hustle for Sports' Day. Do you remember? Well … she has invited me to go to her ballet school when my foot is straighter and I can wear ballet shoes, and I want to go. I think I would like to dance and wear a leotard and a head-band and a tutu and be in a concert. Sometimes at school we do some dancing and I love it. Now you know.' Brianna stopped for a breath.

Max looked at Pam. 'We asked for an idea. I think we got one. Thank you, Brianna. Anything else you want to say?'

'I'm going to bed now, so goodnight Mum. Goodnight Dad. Mum, will you take Dolly out for me tonight please?'

'Clean your teeth, Brianna. Yes. I'll take Dolly out before I go to bed. Goodnight Darling. I'll come and tuck you in in ten minutes.'

Two Tiny, Shiny Echidnas

Victoria Norton

In come the dollars, in come the cents,
to replace the pounds and shillings and the pence.
Be prepared for changes when the coins begin to mix,
on the 14th of February, 1966. (1)

The children's money box was of the printed tin Commonwealth Bank kind, with the bank-building design in colours green and gold, years before Australia adopted the colours as their own. It didn't open unless you used a screwdriver or a hammer; it had a complicated coin slot feature where the coins couldn't be shaken out. They were allowed to put their very occasionally received coins in it. They knew it held at least two sixpences left over from the Christmas cake and they were the most exciting to change over as the children loved the echidna five cent coin they had seen on the ad on TV. Their father had brought a tiny spiky echidna home for them to see once and to hold such a rare and amazing animal made Natasha's dreams begin.

The idea of those wonderful animals being on the coins made wanting one a strong desire. So strong, the two older children, Robert and Natasha, decided to risk their father's wrath. They'd survived earlier punishments so they knew going in what was at stake. The biggest risk was losing the chance to own the lovely new decimal coins.

The small country Convent School the children attended was hosting a man from the Commonwealth Bank. He was to go to the school and change over the old money to the shiny new coins. Robert, as the eldest and being a boy, said he would be in charge of the coins. They kept the secret from their little sisters; they were only six and four and hadn't learned deceit yet.

The screwdriver didn't quite lever the lid off, so Robert grabbed a hammer and in the sweet spot bent the lid enough to shake out the two sixpences – so thin and a dull grey.

In their childish way they thought they could put in two washers from their father's tool box, reclose the lid and they'd never be found out. But of course the lid wouldn't meet all four sides, and the side was dented with a great scratch from the misplaced screwdriver.

They were too far into the adventure to stop there, so they hid the tin in the kitchen cabinet behind the least used dinner set and some raggedy plastic roses.

On the bus to school Natasha squabbled with her brother.

'Why can't I have my own coin?'

In order to make him share she threatened to tell the Nuns, and he reluctantly gave her a sixpence.

'Don't lose it!' he hissed.

They were a composite class of lower primary; Natasha in second class, her brother in third. Their next sister down was Sandra, who was only in kindy and they paid her great attention that day, in case she caught on to the mischief and dobbed. Robert gave her his slice of his mother's juicy fruit cake buttered on one side with butter their mother made, and Natasha held her hand to cross the road from the bus to the school.

A most marvellous gentleman stood at the front of the classroom, wearing a suit and tie. He brought with him a large black bag. Oh! In her excitement Natasha could almost see through the top of the bag into the treasure box full of shiny sparkling new decimal coins..

When the banker finished talking and they'd sung both the jingle and God Save the Queen it was time to swap the money. Natasha didn't remember much of the rest of that day, her joy was in the extreme range, and she skipped down the road from the bus stop to the house after school holding the little coin tight in her fist.

She hid her coin in a hankie in the far corner of her pillowcase. Robert wouldn't tell her where his was hidden. They'd exchange glances and chuckle and their parents would ask: 'What have you two been up to, today?' but they would just smile politely. Natasha harboured some thoughts where from time to time she knew her mother could actually read her mind. Several secrets were exposed by the mother's detecting and Natasha was careful never to let her mother straight in the eye.

It was some time afterwards their thievery was discovered, by whatever bad luck curse their deception had opened.

They had to give up their coins (they never dreamed of using them to buy anything). Whatever physical punishment was metered out it was not out of the normal discipline they got from their father. It's of no consequence now. They had held their gleaming little echidna coins for a time and it was a joyful time from Natasha's childhood regardless of the trouble it caused.

*(1):*Museum of Australian Currency Notes - Dollar Bill Decimal Currency Jingle
http://www.youtube.com/watch?v=kwA64I5SokU

Sunday School Blues

Linda Brooks

My young life was blighted. Our hairdresser must have previously worked for the military. Every day was a bad hair day. I wasn't permitted long hair like most of the other girls. Mum's excuse was that I possessed too many 'cow licks' and this affliction deemed I would spend my life with bad hair days and a short haircut.

I think the real reason was high maintenance manoeuvres necessary for looking after long hair on a pre-schooler were beyond her talents and patience.

Our hairdresser, while not actually using a bowl, managed to give me a bowl haircut every visit—a crooked one at that.

After seeing Pollyanna, I was green with envy. I dreamed about long hair and wide hats with ribbons down the back. I wasn't allowed a hat either. I coped with the shame—most of the time.

While wandering with my brother in our neighbourhood, I didn't think much about it. The kids in our street were predominately boys and my efforts to get them to play with my dolls called down scorn, even though I played with their stupid cars in the dirt with them.

I was often referred to as 'that cute little tomboy' with those who said it never aware of my secret longings for lace gloves, ribbons, socks with bobbles, long hair and darling little purses.

I managed with the embarrassment until The Lord's Day came around. They say religion changes everything. And Sunday School was the place where I stuck out like a sore thumb. After copious begging, tears and promising to be good for the rest of my life, Mum relented and bought a purse.

There would be no compromise on the matter of hair, but it was still a victory. I was soon the proud owner of a purse I'd fallen in love with at first sight.

It was adorable. I sashayed into Sunday school swinging that purse as if I was a model with a thousand dollar designer handbag. I made a great show at offering time, when the basket went down the rows for us to donate our freewill gift to the less fortunate.

I accepted with demure grace all compliments that came my way. Oh the joy!

Pride cometh before a fall. And fall I did.

On the way to the car after the church service Mum looked at me as if something was odd. This wasn't unusual. I adopted my usual nervous chatter aimed at covering any defect that might be glaringly obvious to others, but I didn't have a clue about.

'Where's your purse, Linda?' asked Mum.

My heart sunk to my feet. It was gone. My stomach churned. I hopped from one foot to the other. Tears of despair flowed down my face. At my obvious distress, Mum withheld the lecture that usually accompanied my misdemeanours. We searched the Sunday School building, the road, the church, the gutters and asked the teachers and other children.

I was in agony. Mum, who was renowned for never giving up, finally had to pat my grief stricken face and tell me we couldn't do any more and had to go home. She would contact the church lost property office through the week.

I prayed. Knowing God was more inclined to listen to the

penitent, I began with a list of my faults. This alone made for a long supplication. I then expressed the things I was grateful for, my cat, a warm bed, food, Mummy and Daddy, oh yes, and even my brother although he tormented the life out of me.

I then promised God I would be good for the rest of my life, hoping this impressed Him more than it impressed my mother, who regarded me with dubious looks whenever I made this devout claim to her. I couldn't blame her scepticism, as this dramatic outburst was usually made before a particularly undesirable punishment was in the offing.

All to no avail. I grieved openly and without restraint, throwing myself on my bed. This was something new for me, and Mum was confused by this outpouring of emotion. After much contrition on my part and dire warning on hers, she bought another purse.

It was far less ostentatious. I bravely hid my disappointment. I *would not* throw a tantrum. My one and only attempt at tantrum-throwing brought such a swift and undesirable reaction from my father I'd vowed never to repeat the performance.

I grovelled with gratitude, promising I'd never let it out of my sight. It was only for church; surely I could keep track of it for a few hours a week. But no. The same scenario was repeated the following week. Mum's patience began to wear thin.

'How the blazes can you lose something in such a short time?'

I was as puzzled as she. The harder I tried to remember, the more anxious I became. The more anxious I became, the less I remembered. Disastrously the pattern continued until I was a nervous wreck and Mum had had enough.

'You don't deserve a blooming purse if you can't keep track of it,' she said, upon arriving 'at the end of her tether'. I hung my head. I deserved no less.

This left the problem of where to carry the offering. I was

inclined to forgo the offering basket, but this opinion was not shared by my mother. I was exhorted to think of the less fortunate. I was not inclined to do so. In my opinion *I was* The Less Fortunate. Besides, God had not been forthcoming with helping me find my purses—find my memory, or find any possible thieves who were preying on me (one of my more imaginative scenarios).

My ever practical mother came up with an ideal solution.

Ideal for her.

She tied my offering coins in one of Dad's handkerchiefs and safety-pinned it to the front of my dress for the world to see. Whether she thought humiliation would stimulate my brain, or was simply solving a problem still mystifies me.

There I was; social leper, with a dodgy haircut, no ribbons or bobbled socks, adorned with Dad's hanky and an ugly safety pin.

No matter how strange fashion trends become, this look will never be adopted by any group—Grunge, Goth or otherwise.

Even at four I knew this.

If you haven't already discovered this fact, one of the hardest things to do in a hurry is untie the knot in a handkerchief while the offering basket is approaching ever nearer. Of course the usual nervous memory lapse didn't help, so my last minute panic was seen and snickered at by all.

After this happened a few times I went from humiliation to anger. While walking to the car listening to Mum and Dad bask in the spiritual afterglow of a particularly stirring sermon, I kicked pebbles with the zeal that was missing from my Christian experience.

'Stop that, Linda. You'll ruin your shoes,' said Mum.

'I suppose you'll make me wear Dad's *slippers then!*'

'Don't give your mother cheek,' said Dad. But I caught the glimmer of a curve on his lip. I slowed down and walked a few meters behind them, dragging my feet.

'Keep that up and we'll have a *talk at home*,' said Mum.

'*I'm not wearing Dad's stinking handkerchief again!*' I blustered.

'Oh yes you will!' hissed Mum.

'I wish I was a kangaroo with a pouch!'

(excerpt from 'An Australian Childhood)

Introduction to a Remote Community

Linda Visman

I had arrived in the small Northern Territory community a few days previously, to my first post as a teacher in a remote Aboriginal school. I had met several parents and their children when classes began, and looked forward to meeting more of the community. I had familiarised myself with the ... village, for want of a better word, by driving around its rough rectangle of dirt streets. As I passed each house, its resident pack of dogs ran out, snarling and barking at me and my van. I was amazed to see children, even toddlers, pushing those same dogs around, pulling their tails and hitting them with sticks, all without retaliation from the scrawny, often mangy animals. However, I decided it would be unsafe to walk around the community on my own.

A few families lived in - or rather next to - several rough bough humpies on the edges of the community, but most lived in shacks – I can't call them houses. I soon discovered the poor conditions in these standardised corrugated iron buildings, though I hadn't seen inside them. Each was very basic - a simple rectangular box with one door, a couple of windows and a roof overhang on the door side for verandah. They were more like a large garden shed than a house. Dark green or brown paint coated the outside; the two rooms inside were unpainted. Each shack had a cement slab floor, unlined walls and unglazed windows with a drop-down shutter. They were dark and hot in summer; dark and cold in winter. And often, the inhabitants shared their dwellings with scorpions, centipedes, snakes – the harmless carpet python, the venomous king brown –and red-back spiders.

There was no furniture beyond a few metal bed frames. These almost always stood out in the open air, not far from the small fireplace where the people cooked their meat and damper. The dirty mattresses were piled with a jumble of equally dirty blankets and pillows. By sleeping outside though, they could look up at the endless stars and feel the fresh breeze on their face, instead of stifling in a tin box. The houses had no electricity, no stove or sink or toilet, no bath or shower. There could be anything up to a dozen or more people living at each of these 'camps' as they called them.

Half a dozen old-fashioned long-drop toilet were scattered in open areas between the houses. Three or four other tiny sheds housed single showers. Apart from the families in two new besser-brick houses that had a bathroom and indoor septic toilet, everyone shared these outdoor facilities. They could have a cold shower at any time, but hot showers required someone to light the wood-fuelled chip-heater beforehand. The showers weren't used very often, especially in winter. People usually only washed for something special, perhaps a trip to the clinic, eighty kilometres away, or a meeting with government officials – but not always.

It was pretty rare for the kids to be showered – why bother when they'd soon be dirty again in the dry, red dust? There were no washing machines either, apart from the one at the school. Although some of the women did their washing in tubs or buckets and hung it on barbed wire fences to dry, many wore their clothes until they were very soiled or too worn to hold together. The station store carried good quality clothing – at high quality prices – and that's where people had to go to buy them, as few of them went to town then. Alice Springs was 330 kilometres away, and there were few cars that worked. The purchase of new clothes was one of the major occasions that warranted a shower.

We had a basic ablutions block at school, with an electric hot water system. As part of our health programme, we showered the children before classes every morning. We provided soap, towels and combs, as well as medications for scabies and head lice, both of which were rampant. We also went through hundreds of boxes of tissues each term. Having had five children of my own, I was used to all sorts of messes children can make – from both ends of their bodily systems. However, I wasn't used to the thick yellow or green tramlines that constantly decorated the top lips of these children.

The showers were popular with the little kids, who chattered and squealed as they splashed in the warm water. Sometimes I'd have to go in and get them out, they enjoyed the water so much. The bigger girls took their ablutions seriously, washing their hair with care and combing it before the little mirror in the girls' toilets. The boys over eight or nine years of age weren't so keen on cleanliness. I often had to send them back in when they came out. I'd see, and smell, that they'd only wet their hair instead of putting themselves under the shower and using soap.

Once they were (relatively) clean, all the children changed into the school uniforms we provided: red T-shirts with a black kangaroo motif on front for all of them, with black trousers for the boys and black cotton skirts for the girls. The teachers, or the cleaner if she was there, would then wash the 'camp' clothes and school towels, and hang them on a rope line strung between two large trees behind the ablutions block. The clothes would be dry by the end of the school day, and the kids would change back into them to go home. The teachers would then wash the uniforms again, ready for the next day.

I had been teaching the kids in temperatures above 35°C for several days, and was familiar with the odour of smoke, dogs and bodies that clung to all of them, especially to their hair, even after they had showered. It wasn't unpleasant, just different; certainly not something you'd encounter in average suburban life. We did have an air conditioner that struggled valiantly to inject cooler air into the classroom. It sometimes managed to lower the temperature by as much as ten degrees; thirty degrees was much better to work in than forty. But, of course, the air conditioner didn't work when there was no power, and we'd been having trouble with the school generator from the time we arrived. No generator meant we often had no water as well, as the back-up diesel pump for the bore often broke down too.

Our first parent-teacher meeting was held in the senior (ages eight to thirteen) kids' room, a few days after school started. That's when Alan, the Head Teacher, would formally introduce us 'new mob teachers' and see what direction could be plotted for the term. Alan decided to meet in the classroom instead of under the usual 'meeting trees', because the day was particularly hot and humid. Dark clouds hung over the community, and it looked like they'd release their load at any moment. So, after final bell, the kids changed, we got the uniforms into the washing machine and set up the classroom. It was time to meet the community.

People soon began arriving, trickling across from their houses and through the school gate in a procession of adults, kids and dogs. There seemed to be more dogs than people. Some followed their owners into the classroom, and were either shouted out or kicked away. A couple of vicious dogfights erupted at the door as those being chased out met others who were trying to get in. There was a lot of yelling, until finally, dogs settled outside on the verandah, the meeting could begin. The women sat on the kids' chairs and the men on the desks. Toddlers played around them; babies wailed or suckled; and the adults glanced at us from under black brows and dark unruly hair. They were probably wondering what kind of people this new lot of teachers would be like; they mostly had to suffer whoever the Education Department sent them, though they could refuse anyone a permit to teach or live there if they decided that person was a problem in some way.

As the crowd grew, the air became denser. The odour of one or two people out in the open air is tolerable but, bring twenty or so into a room on a hot day, and the results can be cut with a knife; even though all windows and the door were open, there was no breeze. The acrid smell of unwashed bodies and smoke-laden clothes took my breath away. I found it hard to concentrate on what we were doing there. I took shallow breaths and kept my mouth closed as much as possible. I could see that the other new teacher was having the same problem, though Alan and Allan, who had both worked in communities for some time, seemed oblivious to it.

The meeting went on. We were introduced to the male elders – brothers SM, AM and BM - and told them a little about ourselves. They welcomed us in their quiet way. Alan suggested various plans for the school that met with the approval of all and, before the clouds dropped their load of mid-summer rain, everyone filed out of the classroom. The dogs again noisily asserted their superiority or grovelled their submission and then followed their families back home. The first Parents & Citizens meeting of the year was over.

'I think we'll have the meetings under the shade of the trees next time,' said Alan after the people had left. 'At least the dogs have plenty of room there.'

This is a true story. It was first published as 'Our First Parents' Meeting' in Skive Magazine: Memoirs, Matthew Ward, editor, September 2012.

Suburbia in slumber

Jane McLean

'Closed' signs on café windows advertise a tired Thursday night except for a motley group huddled around the kebab master, greedily succumbing to an oil laden supper, lettuce and beetroot drop rudely in their laps. Another stain blends artistically with already soiled trackie pants.

On the outside they are derelicts of home and duty, lonely they cluster in groups to wait out the night. Shunned by daytime society, the underbelly of this place masks something sinister lurking behind darkened doorways.

At the table he sits, a squatty dishevelled man who looks older than his birth years, and far less wise. Clutching onto his chateau la cardboard as one would a lover; his knobbled fingers trace the edges of the box with adoration. Carrying it tenderly from the local bottle shop, cask dressed in a white plastic 'negligee', stretched taut from the five litre weight. Shamelessly he pulls on the tap and dribbles with pleasure, watching the nectar decant until his cup runneth over. Loudly cursing the waste, he slurps ravenously to dispel theories of half full or half empty. Bringing his goblet to closer inspection he smirks at his innovative drink holder, a crumpled Macca's thick-shake carton lustily retrieved from the council garbage bin.

Slowly slipping the synthetic nightwear from his mistress, his gaze lingers longingly at her name. Moselle, her inner pillow lightened from his gluttonous consumption, is now curvier, softer to his grappling touch.

His words are barely decipherable. Stirred and thickened by the drink his wailing lament begins…

'She should not have hit me. Stupid wife.'

Moselle's hypnotic power draws him to quench his thirst as he unburdens his troubles.

'So I stab her. Three times. There. There. Here,' as his arms gesture the attacks in mid-air, the third to his own shoulder as his arthritic claw latches onto the woollen jumper and twirls it into a knotted ball. He hangs his head and stamps his foot, a dance of demons.

Rising up from his place on the bench seat, he sways to silenced music and mumbles 'jail' and 'judge' over and over again, intermingled with blobs of incoherent words. Six teetering steps he stops and looking into his empty hands, alarm shows on his crinkly chip face. He has forgotten his loved one, orphaned on the seat he had just left. He tries desperately to retrace his steps and fails, taking twice as many to retrieve her than in leaving her. The exercise aborted, he plonks himself down beside her and proceeds to dispense more love juices into his sacred cup.

'Bad,' he berates himself. 'Bad. Bad. Bad.' And then he sobs, rubbing his knuckles into the sockets that birthed the tears. "Judging Judy' will like that I am sorry.' Then he grins as he practices the crying game for the wigged one who will sit in judgement. It becomes a show, a test of dramatics as he turns the volume up and down on the rehearsed remorse.

Tears give way to laughter; a cackle of intent to pervert the course of justice. Egged on by Moselle, ranting of spousal deservedness he blames his wife. Somewhere between the first sip and this swig, his wife ceased being the victim and became the reason for his cruelty.

With venomed voice, he hisses his hate. Emotionally constricted, like the serpent he strikes, lashing out at his one ally, his boxed mistress. Stripping her bare, he brutally rips off her protective clothing, shredding pieces of sodden cardboard then tossing them limply to the ground. In all her glory he holds her naked in his hands, a shimmering silver jewel.

Exhausted, he places her gently beside him, oblivious to her wobble as she nestles snugly into the gaps between the wooden planks of the bench. With a long drawn out sigh, he lays down alongside her, caressing her coldness. His tears have dried up as has his heart. Curled up in a foetal position around his bladdered mistress, drawing her closer, his unshaven face nuzzles into the lover who has given him both joy and sadness.

Eyes heavy, he shuts out the world and succumbs willingly to his drunken trance. A wry smile appears, the nightmare forsaken for a dream. Moselle's juices trickle languidly to the ground, expensing her litres into a pleasure pool under the bench.

She has won.

The self-seeking mistress of the night, his Bella Moselle.

A Tremendous Time

Neridah Kentwell

Vicki sighed as the credits of the Australian colonial-set movie rolled to a close. She didn't want to leave the theatre; she wanted to stay transported back in time, a time that seemed so interesting and romantic. The clothes were so much more elegant then, and the simple way of life so much more appealing. I must have been born too late, she mused.

'Hurry up, blossom,' her husband Tom's voice cut into her daydream, 'I want to get back to feed the animals before dark.'

Once home she still felt a little unreal but decided to get on with the article she was writing, about the people that had first been given the grant of land their hobby farm was now on.

The sun had completely set when Vicki went to use their outside toilet. There was no need to turn on the light, though, as the full moon lit up the whole sky. On the way back up the steps she turned to admire its hugeness. Seeing a falling star out of the corner of her eye, she decided to make a wish.

'Please give me a little time back then, to feel what it was really like,' she whispered, half joking. She turned to go back in and, not concentrating, missed the next step and fell hard on her knee, putting out her hands in the process.

Stunned for a second, she looked down to see she hadn't landed on the usual concrete that formed the back stairs of their house. A rough paver had appeared from nowhere, beneath her. I must have hit my head as well, she thought as she shook it, and then painfully stood up, pushing her mane of hair back off her face.

Her eyes widened when she saw what was in front of her - a short sandstone path leading up to an early Australian settler's cottage, complete with shingled roof. The front door stood open and a flickering light came from inside.

A feeling of panic threatened to overwhelm her - everything was so unfamiliar. But taking a deep breath she ventured forward, reassuring herself it couldn't last. I must be fantasising, so I may as well enjoy it while I can, she thought. Limping a little from her sore knee, Vicki stepped in.

She found herself inside a single room that could be no more than six metres long, with slab walls and a low ceiling of hessian bags. An open fireplace at one end had a small fire burning, over which hung a huge, blackened kettle with steam gently escaping from the spout. The stocky wooden table and matching solid chairs took up a lot of the area. She could smell the smoke and hot water vapour as well as another scent she couldn't detect. Then she remembered. Vinegar! That's what it is. They used a lot of vinegar in this period, I know, for cleaning.

I can't be dreaming this, thought Vicki, as she ran her hand over the roughly made table, almost getting a splinter stuck in her ring finger. How could she be dreaming, if she could feel every fault in the dark wood that probably came from a huge felled red cedar? It was nothing like her smoothly polished pine kitchen table at home.

Vicki peeked behind a curtain set across a corner of the room. 'Oh, look at the bed linen!' She spoke out loud, enthralled, staring at the hand sewn patchwork quilt on the four poster bed.

'And the nightwear!' She reached out reverently to touch a long sleeved, white cotton nightgown with carefully pin-tucked yoke. She realised her dirty, though hardly grazed hands, and damaged knee, would need a wash first, so she went back out to the rainwater trough she'd noticed on the way in.

Reassured she wouldn't bleed on the clothing, her fascination overcame her feeling of trespassing as she felt an urgent need to be part of it. Carefully going through the few female clothes that were folded neatly in a camphor chest with its lid left open, at the base of the bed, Vicki chose the more worn of the long dresses and put it on. It fit her perfectly. The scraping of boots at the back door brought Vicki quickly back to reality.

To Vicki's surprise her husband stood in front of her. But not her husband as she knew him; he appeared more tanned and muscled. He also had a full chestnut beard, which was long and apparently uncut for some time, like his matching hair. Very unlike her clean shaven, short haired Tom.

The man was staring at her in consternation. 'Victoria, please don't upset me again! I've come in to find no food on the table, the third time this week!'

Vicki suddenly realised how this 'husband', apparently of the late 18th or early 19th century, viewed her, and decided it would be best to humour him for now. Who knew where the real Victoria was? Nodding, she went to put on the calico apron she could see hanging on a hook on the wall.

'Um, Tom,' she asked, heart thumping, 'Can you remind me if we've got any cold meat and salad anywhere?'

He looked at her with concern, 'You know I was christened Thomas, Victoria, and you also well know where our food is kept out the back! I do not know what has got into you lately. I think I'll have to see what Reverend Smith has to say on Sunday, after church.'

Vicki cautiously ventured out behind the house and another revelation unfolded, illuminated by the same bright moon she'd left behind. In front of her must have been at least an acre of vegetables, over 4000 square metres, interspersed with flowers and herbs. As she grew some vegetables herself at home, she knew how much work was involved. Further out there were fruit trees galore, and she was sure she could see a cow in a nearby paddock. *I hope I'm not expected to milk it in the morning*, she worried.

After a quick inspection, she found some salted meat in a tiny stone outhouse. While freshly picking everything for the salad, she noticed some of the varieties were definitely unfamiliar.

'Time for bed,' Thomas announced, stretching and yawning in what seemed like only minutes. When he went outside for a wash in the same trough she had used earlier, Vicki quickly changed into the beautiful nightdress. She pondered the position she was in, having to get into bed with a strange man. But what choice did she have?

Luckily, as soon as Thomas climbed in, he rolled over and was asleep in seconds. Vicki lay awake for some time, trying to plan what she could do. She eventually fell asleep just as she heard a rooster starting the first of his early morning calls.

The sun beamed heat through the window, waking Vicki. She felt groggy and strange. Her neck and knee hurt. She rubbed a crumpled ear, but suddenly sat up and laughed.

Thank goodness, she thought, it was just a dream; it had felt so much like I was actually there. I must have fallen asleep with my head on the desk. That explains why my neck and ear hurt. The last thing I remember is falling on the paver.

Looking down to rub her knee, she let out a tremendous scream. She was still wearing Victoria's nightdress!

Parlez vous francais?

Linda Ruth Brooks

I survived the first month on the Female Medical Ward and the domination of Sister Renshaw. Just. While not actually succumbing to complacence, I was feeling a little more comfortable. My next roster rotation was on Surgical I, which was devoted to general surgery patients. I was beginning to feel like a nurse and would soon shed the dreaded 'Blue Bags' that signified our newness to the world.

I was even beginning to feel a little pride in myself. And we all know what they say about *that*.

I arrived on the ward for the am shift early; feeling bright-eyed, bushy-tailed and at peace with the world. I showered and prepared a gentle little woman for a radical mastectomy and attended several other patients. When we were at morning tea in the staff room the charge sister approached us and asked if anyone spoke French.

My tiny bosom swelled with self-importance. I had done five years of high school French and enjoyed it passionately. I had read Parisian Magazines, read Albert Camus' novel' L'Etranger', watched French films on excursions to Metropolitan theatres and visited with my French teacher and his garrulous family, joining in their conversations.

I was up for this task.

There was a French speaking Mauritian woman who was post-operative and deeply distressed and there was no family member present to interpret for her. So off I went to save the day.

She was a tiny woman who had the vocal capacity of an opera singer. Her tightly curled black hair stood on end and gave her a surprised look. She was brandishing the nurse call bell, shaking it as if it was a weapon. I responded with my best French, interspersed with English whenever I lost the plot. Which was a little more often than I expected.

'Oui, um Madame, vous desirez, um, a nurse, um, et je suis ici, um, to, um vous aidez.' I sighed with some satisfaction.

Grossly *unfounded* satisfaction as it transpired.

I immediately discovered that people who are *not* helping you learn the language, have a lot less patience with you than those hired to teach it to you. They also speak at the speed of light. Only the accent resonated; not one single word sounded familiar.

The only phrases that seemed to have stuck in my swelled head were simple ones of greeting or asking directions to regions in Paris.

It was at this point that I realised the formality of asking 'comment ca va?' (How are things going?) was not only completely inadequate it appeared to be a downright insult. 'Things' were obviously *not* going well and the woman conveyed with eloquent gestures that I was an idiot for asking thank you very much.

She continued to shake the call bell menacingly.

The next phrases that came to mind were how to ask for directions to the railway station and enquire 'mon frère, ou est la plume de ma tante' (my brother, where is my auntie's pen?) I also uselessly remembered how to request the location of the local 'gendarmerie' (police station).

Apparently the school curriculum was designed for students with artistic and cultural leanings and would only ever need travel vocabulary. None of our French classes even vaguely covered the possibility that one might need to enquire about constipation, difficulty with urination, levels of pain or any other conditions that might relate to physical symptoms or disease processes.

Trying to remember the marvellous essays I had written in French and thought magnificent at the time only hurt my head. My silent agony caused the woman in the bed to repeat frantically whatever it was that she wanted; still waving the call bell, with an increasingly strident voice.

In the true style of the obsessive perfectionist, I would not give up. So I started a mime sequence that would have done credit to Marcel Marceau.

Unfortunately, I then faced the problem that some of the things I might want to ascertain could possibly look a little obscene to the uninformed and were sure to insult this poor woman if I was off the mark.

Which I apparently was. Repeatedly.

When her level of distress rose to fever pitch, I thought it wise to leave the room as graciously as possible, because it began to dawn on me that I was actually increasing her frustration and ire.

As I left the room, she threw the water jug at my retreating back, and then spoke the only French I understood that day.

'Imbecile!'

Birthday Boy

Louise Elizabeth

It was cold but not raining. That stopped last night. Since the flood, I get kind of unsettled when it's wet for very long. Mum said the fluttering feeling in my stomach is known as butterflies. I asked her how they got inside but she told me to stop being so literal. The sound of rain on the tin roof over the verandah used to make me feel warm, but now I don't know if it's going to go on and on, and the river will flood. A new bridge is being built, but I'm not sure that will stop the flood next time. The house only smells bad when it rains for a while. Mum said she wanted to live on top of a hill. I told her there are no hills here. She said there are in other places.

Pete was having a birthday and Mum decided it was time we went to the country for a picnic. Uncle Tom was coming down from Sydney and he was bringing our cousins to play with us. Such excitement. We hadn't seen them for a few years. Last year, we stayed at home for Christmas. Mum said it was because of the floods but I didn't understand how that affected travel. I think she just didn't want to see Dad.

We went in two cars. Our aunt drove our car. She's does it better than Mum. We don't jerk around as much and she doesn't pray all the time.

We stopped by the river's edge. There was a special place to cook. Rocks piled into a circle, with a grate on top.

Mum frowned and said to Uncle Tom, 'Are you sure that's clean?'

He said, 'Don't worry. The fire will get rid of any germs.'

I said, 'What germs are those?'

Mum said, 'Go and play.'

No one ever answers my questions.

It was such fun running around. There were lots of logs to jump over. Aunt Beatrice kept the pests amused, so I didn't have to worry about being a good big sister. I ran faster that my cousin. All that practising must have helped.

'Come on. Time to wash up for lunch.'

Mum had brought a thermos filled with soapy water. She wet a facecloth and we all had to get cleaned up. Mum always worries about germs. I've never seen any so I don't know what's she's on about.

Uncle Tom had put potatoes into the ashes. He offered me one but it was all black so I shook my head.

'You don't know what you are missing?'

I turned up my nose. 'It looks burnt.'

'You don't eat the black bit, silly.' He cracked one open. 'You eat what's inside.' He scooped some of the flesh out with a fork and held it towards me. 'Taste it.'

I was going to refuse but then I saw my younger sisters watching me. After all, I was the eldest girl. I took the fork. Not bad. After my brave example, the others wanted to taste as well. I felt smug, when Uncle Tom said, 'Good girl.'

After we had eaten everything there was still some bread in the picnic basket so Uncle Tom asked, 'Who wants to make toast?'

I'd done that before, so I left the little ones to get their faces red. Pete, my cousins and I went back to climb the tree hanging over the river.

We had all chosen a branch to sit on, and throw sticks and bark into the water. The river was flowing over the rocks, and the sticks kept on getting caught in rocks.

My cousin Roger yelled, 'I've got a stone. I'll see if I can hit that stick.' He stood up to get a better view. As he did, he overbalanced, and grabbed a branch to keep his balance but it broke off, knocking Pete off his perch and onto the ground. I screamed.

Mum and Uncle Tom ordered us to climb down.

Roger kept on saying, 'It's not my fault.'

I glared at him. 'Yeah, whose fault is it then?'

Pete looked a funny colour. He clutched his left arm. He had tears in his eyes. Pete never cried not even when ….

'I'll take him to the hospital.' Uncle Tom lifted Pete up, carried him to our car, and put him in the back seat. Mum went with him.

We were left to do the cleaning up and then we all had to get into Aunt Beatrice's car. It wasn't as big as ours, but she told us to squash in as best we could. Roger got to sit in the front with his mother and his sisters.

Aunt Beatrice told me. 'Stop it, Anne. Blaming Roger won't help.'

'But if he …'

'These things happen.'

Roger couldn't help himself. 'Just like Mum says, it wasn't my fault.'

She said, 'Roger, be quiet. We'll talk later.'

The journey home continued in silence.

I never trusted my cousin again.

The Apple Orchard

Helen Marshall

I sat on the old rutted tree stump Dad used for chopping wood. I felt every scar through my jeans. The air was still and dense with fog. The orchard hid beyond my limited orb of vision, standing in soldier rows. Waiting patiently for my last inspection.

I pulled my gum boots and socks off, and plunged my feet into the frosty grass. A shock surged through me as icy tentacles ran up my body. I stepped out onto the worn track between the trees, wanting all my senses to remember. Instinct guided me.

Thousands of days directed my steps. The passage of feet had worn the track smooth and its texture guided my soles. Brittle leaves crunched and crumbled under my feet, returning to the earth.

I was twelve and the orchard was the only home I'd known. Tomorrow we'd be leaving to start a new life in the city. The shattering decision to leave the mountains had left me totally adrift. All that I knew was here, and I loved every part of it.

I wanted to record my home with every sensation I possessed. The sight of it was already imprinted on my brain. I'm sure the other senses were too, but I needed to be certain.

The pungent smell of early windfall fruit and damp earth drifted around me, in conflict with the fresh tartness of nearly ripe apples. Why was Dad moving now? The apples were nearly ripe! It didn't make sense. But he had told us of his mother's need to have her son close by. She was ailing and afraid. Illness was gnawing at her body and mind. She couldn't face it alone, and there was no-one else.

A strong rope of cobweb pulled at my exposed cheek. I knew that feeling: an orb weaver was the only spider to spin such strength. I instinctively pulled back. I didn't want to ruin her night's dew-hung weaving: so I ducked and moved on.

The white air was still. Perfectly still and hushed. Distant sounds were hard to locate. Birds chattered softly, high up in the surrounding gums.

An unseen visitor nibbled secretly at a fallen apple. I couldn't tell if it had two legs or four.

I held my face up to the faint nebulous glow of the morning sun. A tiny zephyr drifted across my face, almost imaginary, tickling a strand of hair.

The leaves touched each other with muted leathery slaps as I reached out and ran my hands through the heavily laden branches. The colours and shapes I knew so well brought the scene to my unseeing eyes.

I walked slowly to the end of the row and stood there breathing in the fresh cold air. Puffs of warm breath plumed and vanished. The skin on my face tingled and tightened.

I knew I would never experience this again. It had to last me for a lifetime. My future loomed before me, unseen, unknowable and vaguely ominous.

I sit here now at eighty-three and remember those well recorded impressions. My sight is nearly gone, but my other senses still function adequately.

I was wrong about never experiencing the apple orchard again. Every time I crunch into a fresh juicy apple (these days cut into small manageable slices), those parting moments in the mist flood back to my mind, and I relive them with the vigour and simplicity of youth.

First Impressions

Linda Visman

Charmaine wasn't nearly as pretty as her name. With dark hair and features, she was stocky in build, and her clothes looked like they came from the cheapest racks of the Op Shop. It was hard to tell her age. Maybe fifty, I thought, seeing a few strands of grey. She'd suddenly stopped at my front fence.

'Am I going the right way to the shops?'

She sounded tentative. I looked up at her and smiled. I understood being shy.

'Yes, you are. Turn left at the crossroads. The shops are right there.'

'Thanks. I've just moved here and wasn't sure of the way.'

She smiled and her whole appearance was transformed. Her smile lit up her eyes and brightened her slightly lop-sided features, making them interesting instead of unattractive. She looked at my son, riding his trike on the driveway.

'How old is your boy? He looks about the same age as my daughter.'

'Geoff's four - my youngest. All the others are at school.'

We chatted for several minutes, exchanging family details. She had two sons and a daughter, and her family had just come to the city from Nyngan. As she left, I threw out the invitation.

'It's hard being in a new place when you don't know anyone. Come any time. Maybe the kids can play together.'

'Yes, perhaps.' Her smile was uncertain.

My friend, Anne, was appalled when I told her about Charmaine, especially when I said I'd invited her to visit.

'You're joking! She's an Abo. They're troublemakers. Her kids must be the new ones at the school. I've heard they're a problem.'

I asked my kids about them when they came home from school. My eleven-year-old was casual.

'Yeah, Kyle's in my class. He doesn't do anything much, except draw pictures – he's good at that. Him and his little brother stick together at Recess.'

'Damon's in my class,' eight-year-old Paul added. 'There's a little sister too, but she doesn't come to school.'

In the next weeks, I saw Charmaine walk past a few times, but she never called in. I supposed she was too shy or too busy. I knew they were still around at least, as Paul mentioned how Kyle and Damon were still not joining in. I told my boys they could help by being friendly towards them.

'I like Kyle. His pictures are great - 'specially the animals.'

'Yeah, Damon's real good at drawing too.'

I wondered why those two lads were so quiet. Was something wrong at home? Did Charmaine need support? I didn't really want to get involved if there was trouble.

My husband said I shouldn't pre-judge people. He suggested I take our youngest for a walk by Charmaine's place. Maybe she'd appreciate some company, and her daughter could play with Geoff. I'd learned where she lived, so it was just a matter of getting up the courage. When Paul told me the boys hadn't been at school for most of the week. I decided to go the next day.

As we approached Charmaine's house, I could see several cars parked outside. Charmaine and two boys were at the front door. I couldn't see her daughter. A dark-haired man stood on the grass – her husband? Other adults stood around the front yard, and a dozen kids of all ages played among them.

Looks like she has plenty of people after all, I thought. *I should have known an Aboriginal family wouldn't be left alone. I needn't have worried about her.*

I felt like an intruder. I had just decided to turn back, when Charmaine looked across and saw me. She came to the gate to meet me, a smile on her face.

'Hello.'

'Hi. Thought I'd call by and see how you've settled in, but it looks like you have company.'

'That's all right. I haven't had time to drop in, but I wanted to say thank you.'

'What for?' I was puzzled.

'Your boys have been real nice to Kyle and Damon at school. It's been good to have someone stick up for them and not call them names like the others. They've had a hard time lately.'

I was amazed. I hadn't realised her boys were being harassed – or that mine had defended them. Charmaine went on.

'I'd really like it if you could join us. You can meet my husband. We're about to have a celebration of our daughter's life.'

'Your daughter's life?'

'Oh, didn't you know? Chantelle had advanced leukaemia. That's why we came here – for the hospital. She passed away on Monday. We've just come back from the funeral. Now we're going to give thanks for our wonderful little girl.'

The therapist

Mary Gabb

Although there were three doctors in the small country town, Mrs W., well known for her wide knowledge of complaints and their 'natural' cures, would not dream of consulting one of them. She had given up on doctors when they failed to diagnose or manage the illness of her two year-old daughter. She had consulted all of them before she lost confidence in the medical fraternity; taken advice from one, and one week later had the prescribed treatment reversed by another.

As the fount of medical knowledge, or of anything else for that matter, she had written them all off. She knew one of them was having an affair with his receptionist nurse who was also the local pastor's daughter; the other was a Catholic with whose religion Mrs W. emphatically disagreed. The third did not inspire confidence—he was overweight and she knew about the mistakes he had made.

Unofficially, Mrs W. acted as an unauthorized alternative medical advisor to anyone who wanted to listen. Although she had no radio or TV she had two books in her home library, consulted so frequently, that she almost knew the contents from back to front. *The Home Physician*, and *Back to Eden* were her unfailing sources of information. She also entered into correspondence with medical experts all over the world and received excerpts from scientific papers and journals which she read avidly. She correctly diagnosed diphtheria in a visiting child, by matching the coloured picture in her Home Physician to the spotty lesions she saw in the child's throat—and her reputation in the neighbourhood grew.

She had herself, tried several dietary therapies; carrots were purchased by the sack; grated, squeezed by hand through muslin daily and made into carrot juice. Then followed the citrus and the grape juice cures. Sweet black grapes were picked by the bucketful from the vine which clambered over the roof of the garage, and was turned into dozens of bottles of thick dark grape-juice. In March her home smelled like a winery, and visitors were treated to a sampling of her therapeutic brew. She swore by these healing elixirs.

'You can feel it doing good as it goes down,' she claimed.

Traditional home therapies were an extension of Mrs W's dietary cures. Boils needed no doctor to treat them; bread and soap poultices were strapped into position on the offending affected area, left on overnight, and in the morning the angry lesion had given up its crater of puss to the bandage. The painful boil gradually subsided over a couple of days.

Paronychia (whitlows) were treated with hot and cold foments, disappearing after only a couple of treatments. Painful joints were also found to respond well to hot and cold foments. And the magical therapeutic benefit of honey was demonstrated to be far cheaper and superior to a doctor's visit. A spoon of honey applied to sores and ulcers, left undisturbed for several days, produced remarkable results; thus she advised anyone who complained of the smallest infection, scratch or ulcer. Astonishingly, recalcitrant ulcers which had been troubling friends and relatives for months, disappeared without the services of a doctor. A very convenient cure, since her husband was the town's only apiarist.

The garlic therapy was notable for its dramatic curative powers, and side effects! Garlic could be crushed and applied to persistent lesions, discoloured spots and skin cancers.

After taking the garlic advice from Mrs W., one trusting friend complained tearfully in an angry telephone call that the treatment had taken all the skin off her nose, leaving it as raw as a freshly butchered steak. 'Never tell anyone to do that again!' she warned. But after it had healed and new skin had grown over the meaty nose, her treating doctor could find no trace of the offending skin cancer, and the operation to remove it was cancelled. An abject apology was offered and accepted, and Mrs W. happily continued to recommend the garlic treatment.

We seem to be a panicky lot, this sophisticated society of ours. Perhaps the burgeoning medical budget of today could become manageable if some of these home remedies were widely promoted ... and applied.

The Flood

Louise Elizabeth

It had been raining for days. Sally, our mother's helper, nagged us to put our toys on the table so they wouldn't get wet. I sneered at her with the wisdom of a seven-year old with younger siblings.

'Don't be silly. It never floods here.'

Her dark eyes flashed. I wondered if I had gone too far.

'Anne, do as you are told.'

I opened my mouth for a retort, but my older brother Pete nudged me and said out of the corner of his mouth, 'Better do it or Dad …'

He didn't have to say anything else.

Sullenly, I obeyed and ordered the younger ones to follow my lead. Sally looked on sardonically. I'm sure she overheard what Pete said to me.

Sally lived with us, and now Martha and her daughter Claudia had come to stay. Martha helped Mum in the house. Claudia went to school with us. I didn't like that but Mum told me to stop being a snob.

When she first came, I thought she might be a friend as I only had an older brother and then two younger brothers. My sisters were too young to talk properly. The very first week, I was in the backyard playing with my brothers up and down the woodheap, running around the house, and then having a swing. We all got hot and sweaty, and a little dirty. Well it wasn't really my fault that I fell in the chook pen. I mean, I was being chased and took a short cut. How was I to know the henhouse had been weakened when we took some planks to build a cubby house in the mandarin tree? One side of the henhouse collapsed, and I fell among squawking hens.

Sally ran out to see what was wrong. Did she show me any sympathy? No. After she had finished yelling at me, we had to dismantle our cubby and help her repair the henhouse. She urged us to hurry before Mum came home.

As I walked inside to clean up, Claudia looked me up and down. 'In my country, girls behave like ladies and not rednecks.'

I only whacked her lightly but she cried as though I had really fought her. *What a weakling.* I knew then she'd never be my friend. *I hate crybabies.*

Her mother said, 'Zis is not the way to behave mein kind.'

I stared at her open-mouthed. *What was she talking about?*

Sally came in and hustled me to the bathroom. I only just got dressed before my parents arrived.

We had been cooped up for a week. No school. No playing outside, and now out toys were piled on the table. How was I supposed to find the one I wanted? Mum said, 'Read a book.'

I ask you. *How many books can you read before it gets boring?*

We all sat around the dinner table. Sally ate with us but Martha and Claudia ate by themselves in the kitchen. Dad was home, so the conversation at the dinner table was only about passing things like salt. We all remembered to say please. When the meal was over, Dad said, 'I'm going to Sydney. I'll be there for a while.'

We looked at him wide-eyed. Great! Mum didn't seem to happy but then she seldom did.

Dad got up from the table. 'Be good for your mother.' He walked out of our lives.

'Why is Dad going to Sydney?'

Mum glared at me. 'I think it is time you all went to bed. Sally, will you please help them.'

Sally stood up.

'Mum, are you going to read us a story?'

She stared at me and then blinked. 'No, not tonight.'

Sally took us upstairs.

That night it rained and rained. Harder than it had been. There were flashes of lightning and thunder boomed, causing windows to rattle. I was glad I was brave. I didn't whinge when my younger sisters came into my bed for comfort.

The next morning, the rain had stopped. I thought great; we can now go out and play. I ran down the hallway but someone had put a chest of drawers across the top of the stairs. I started to climb over it when Sally shouted, 'Stop.'

I turned.

'You can't go down.'

'Why not?'

'It's flooded.'

Peter had joined me and we both peered over the balustrade and caught glimpses of water. How exciting. Sally rushed over and pulled us back.

'Don't do that. You could fall.'

'But I want to see,' I whinged.

'Get dressed.'

'But …'

'For once in your life, just do as you are asked.'

Sally sounded so strict, I obeyed her.

'I know,' Pete whispered in my ear. 'We can look over the balcony.'

'But that's Dad's room.'

'He's not here.'

Good thinking. We tiptoed down the hallway. We could hear Sally talking to the younger children and slid past their room. My heartbeat raced as Pete tried the door to Dad's room. We eased our way in. I stopped in amazement. None of Dad's things were on his dressing table. I looked at Pete but he just shrugged. We opened the door to the balcony and we stepped outside. My jaw dropped. As far as the eye could see, there was water. Not clear blue but muddy with things floating in it. I saw a dead cow and bits of fencing.

As we watched, a police boat roared along the street and stopped at our house. A policeman climbed out, reached back and lifted Mum out. She carried a bulging pillowcase. We heard him say, 'Now don't worry, Mrs M. We'll bring more food for you and the young ones if you run out. Please don't try and cross the road again until the waters are gone.'

Mum's prim voice floated up to us. 'Thank you, officer. You've been most kind.'

She carried the pillowcase inside and I heard her talking to Martha.

We had to stay upstairs for days. I ask you. We soon got bored watching the people struggle in the floodwaters. Sally yelled at us, saying the balcony wasn't safe. We played board games, guessing games and had stories read to us.

The floodwaters eventually receded, leaving stinking mud

behind. Our next excitement was watching the miners come into the house with shovels as wide as my outstretched arms. They took away the mud but Mum said it wasn't safe for us and we were sent away in buses to other people's homes.

I cried each night until I got home again.

Mum was so unsympathetic. She stood there glaring at me.

'Just do as you are told. Look around. All the children are going away because you might get sick.'

My brother Peter had already left. I just didn't want to go by myself. New things are fun but I always had someone I knew nearby.

'But ...'

'Do you have to argue about everything?'

Mum glanced at my younger siblings, lining up in pairs near different buses. 'They are doing what they are told.'

My lower lip trembled, but I could see from the look in Mum's eye she wasn't going to give in. I gave a theatrical sigh and climbed into the waiting bus. I dutifully turned back and waved as the bus eased its way out of town. Just past the wheat silos, it turned right, and then along a road I'd never travelled. In a way, I was glad to get away from home. It smelt. The miners had taken out the carpet, and the mud, but the walls and floor were still clammy to the touch. The backyard was starting to crack as the mud dried. Mum wouldn't let us go outside because it was dangerous, or so she said. I had only tripped three times and my brother, Peter, only once caught his foot and fell onto his face. His nose bled. Mum yelled.

Sally, the women who used to help Mum look after us had left. She told Mum, 'I'm not staying in a smelly place like this a moment longer.' That wasn't true. She was still in the house for another two days because the trains weren't moving. So like a grown-up to lie. Pity Martha and Claudia didn't go too. I said that to Mum but she told me I was a very selfish child. It was hard enough to get people to help when there were so many children and I should be nice so they wanted to stay. I stared at her. I mean, what work was she going on about? I got myself dressed and helped my little sisters, sometimes. What else was there to do?

Now here I was, the last child in the bus. Everyone else had been dropped off along the way. I eased myself to the front of the bus.

'How much longer?'

'Now Annie, don't fret. We'll soon be there. You'll like it. He's a schoolteacher.'

'My name is Anne, not Annie.'

'Hoity-toity.'

I glared at his eyes in the rear vision mirror, and sat back, staring at the countryside.

Life is so unfair. You would think a schoolteacher would have a nice home, or at least a toilet inside. No. You had to go down the back and into a spider infested little room. It was so far from the house. They used torn up newspaper. I sat down there and cried. How could Mum have been so cruel?

I had to share a room. I know they were kind to let me stay, Mum had told me this so often, but they were so strange. I hoped I could go home tomorrow. Surely, the sickness would have gone by then.

It got worse. In the middle of the night, I heard a strange sound. It sounded like someone going to the toilet. I sat up in bed. The other girl, Helen, was sitting on a pot in the room. She pushed it under the bed.

'If you want to go, you can use this too.'

I stared at her, then slid down in the bed and pulled the covers over my head. There is no God. In the middle of the night, I crept out of the house. I was busting. I went on the grass.

When we were having breakfast the next day, Mr Thomas said,

'Don't go outside at night. There are snakes.'

'But …'

'Don't argue with me. Now eat up and we'll go over to the school.'

'School – I don't have my books.'

'I'll give you one.'

The rest of breakfast was eaten in silence.

They didn't wear a proper school uniform. I had to wear Helen's old tunic but my blouse wasn't white. It had flowers on it. I felt uncomfortable but when I got to the school, everyone wore something different. There were long benches at long tables. Each table was a different class. This one room had little kids, and big kids, and everyone in between. It was so noisy.

Mr. Thomas gave me a piece of paper.

'Here fill this in. It'll let me know what work to give you.'

I took it. It had lots of questions, all different types. I filled it in, and put up my hand.

'Well done.' He looked down. 'I see you've printed your answers. Don't you know how to write?'

Someone sniggered. Mr Thomas's eyes raked the room. 'Get on with your work.' He looked back at me. 'Do you want to learn how to write?'

My heart raced. Do it before everyone else at my school? Yeah.

He gave me a sheet of paper. 'Trace these letters. The arrows show you which way to use the pencil. I'll show you.'

Wow. This is so hard. I think I'll keep printing.

'Think how proud your parents will be when they see you can write. You'll be such a big girl.'

If I never saw Dad again, how will he know I can write? I felt a tear come to my eye but I blinked it away. I was not going to cry in front of strangers. I concentrated on thinking about Mum, and how the younger kids would be so impressed.

I stayed there for two long weeks. I was so glad to get home. I tried to be nice to everyone for at least a couple of days.

The Headland

Victoria Norton

I have a secret place. It's a short walk from the clearing where I park my car, in a scrubby spot overlooking the lake. I call it the Headland and I come here to play my flute.

I thought I was the only person to spend time here, but today I found cigarette butts and empty peach vodka mix bottles so it is likely a teenage retreat. Somewhere they can defiantly test their boundaries. Just as I do.

It's been so much effort just to get here. The twins whinged when I dropped them at day care, and my boss didn't believe I was really sick. I'm taking a sickie from Robert as well. Sarah and Rubin are only three, and it's going to take forever for them to be grown and gone. I wince as I consider that I don't enjoy motherhood like I'm expected to, but I might as well be honest with myself – I need a break from them too.

A sandstone block makes a clearing where I can sit cross-legged. It's not quite level and as I set down the wine bottle, it falls. I grab at it and miss. The bottle I took from the back of Robert's cellar cracks open. Damn. What a waste of an expensive red.

Native shrubbery surrounds this space and you can eat the sweet gum from the silky-oak here– it's a little like chewing gum. There are some little straggling plants that have lolly-like fruit in the spring; a pink lilly-pilly, an orange kangaroo apple and the purple fruits of the native grape. The outcropping that makes this a headland contains an age old midden of oyster, mussel and cockle shells, broken by time and bleached chalky white by the sun. The bunya pine was a bonus for the first inhabitants many centuries ago, linked with seasonal feasts of ripe fruits, bunya nuts and shellfish.

He is of the Currawong... He asked permission of the guardians to enter the forest, to bring me with him. He sang a secret, sacred song, then whirling and swirling from above came the answering cloud of shimmering blue black backs, and I fell on my knees to the ground, but softly, feeling the earth pulse in time with my breath, Currawong...'I am of the Currawong people,' a hundred wings in rhythm and song, so sweet, so thrilling, the sharp sandy earth on my face so starkly contrasting with the soft feathered whoosh of white flashed wings. Leaving, he held my hand and took me, 'Currawongggg...'

I have lessons and sheet music and I practise my instrument every day. Painstakingly, so I get my husband's money's worth. Purposefully, so the children know to leave me this half-hour free from their twinned wanting.

The flute begins as three pieces of silvery sculpture that when joined become *My Precious*, my beautiful escape machine. I start by creating mournful trills and phrases, the notes long and low. The water's gentle splash, in and out, is a soothing sound. I mimic with my music the breath-like movements of the lake rising and collapsing, rising and collapsing.

My fingers fly with renewed vigour and it becomes an allegro sonata by Handel. The grey-green canopy of the vegetation catches the wind in the slender foliage, flicking the needles as it passes, making a reverent shushing sound of encouragement. The greenery surrounds the clearing like velvet curtains in a concert hall, and the mat of needles underfoot swallows the sound.

The intricate music of my flute solo spins out melodic sound lines, alive with tone and texture, and it becomes a physical form, a wave of sound, wrapping around me, merging, melding, mending me to this place. Bright and rich, my sound colours the atmosphere. Purple. Emerald. Gold. It is the Aurora Australis. I am the concert flutist. I am the conductor. I am the audience. The applause is mine.

Today the lake offers a palette of grey with silver flashes and tea rinsed edges. It reflects low hung clouds pregnant with showers. Where the land meets the salty waters are some rocks, fallen and smashed. It is difficult to climb down but I do, determined to clean up the rubbish collected there. I slide a little and set off a flurry of dirt and stone.

Down on the shore a small blue swimmer crab keeps nipping at me as I work to untangle it from some fishing line. He mistakes me for a predator and strikes at my thumb, so I reluctantly let him go. I'd have to break his nipper claws to save him and I can't do that. He is trapped – just as I am.

Close to shore a pod of pelicans snap-happily gorges on bream. I slip on the slimy rocks as I pick up rubbish discarded by humans and rejected by the lake. I'm balancing gawkily with my arms outstretched, like a pelican's bedraggled wings on landing.

My nostrils flare at a sudden bad smell. A bloated porcupine fish floats in to view, skin sloughing off in pieces with the movement of the water. It tumbles in a clumsy half turn and floats off. The bad odour remains.

I find a child's sole-less sports shoe, made in a far away factory by a shoe-less child working for a soul-less company. The same sort my children wear. There is a soft drink bottle with a piece of garden hose attached – a homemade bong, lost over the edge of the Headland, by out -of -it teens. I rip out strips of torn plastic from the embattlement of seagrass and sand. Plastic that will not biodegrade – just become millions of ever-smaller pieces destroying the seascape and all life within it.

I shove the rubbish into a rusted chocolate drink tin, and I clamber awkwardly back up the bank. The high calorie drink is made by a company with shares in a diet product. They recycle their own bio-feedback network of fat and thin, and make money in both directions. I wonder will my children lay waste to their environment; they certainly leave a mess at home. I feel a panic rising and I think our planet is running out of time.

I'm about half way up the bank, when, out of the corner of my eye, I spot a bright yellow bauble, bobbing at the edge of the water. I can't sit up on the Headland with garbage below me, so I shuffle back down to check it out.

The weight of an iron key pulls the plastic float under the water.

The key is strange, quite large and heavy. It looks more like my grandmother's door key than the kind of key used to secure the cabin of a small yacht or cruiser. It has a single flat tooth, a cylindrical shank and the part you hold is shaped like the number eight. It isn't rusty so it hasn't been in the water very long.

The plastic float has some words and numbers etched into it. I can make out 'All–ro 5-78.' I'm not sure what it means. Perhaps it's a mooring number. My mind fills with romantic visions of Johnny Depp, pirates, maps and treasure chests. *Furl the mainsail, scrub the deck, a barrel of rum, a drunken song, swords clash and gunfire flash and canon boom and decks creak, walk the plank and scrub the deck me hearty.* I laugh at myself. Get real. Still, I keep the key. The mystery has captured something in me, given me a feeling of hope that I might work out the riddle, and by doing this I might sort out the other puzzles in my life. Like why did he cheat on me? And will he do it again?

Blast. I've cut my hand on the tin. I wrap my hankie around the rush of blood. Anxiety fills me and I sulk. I'm at risk of infection, of tetanus. Will I need stitches? Will it affect my flute playing? I'll have to see a doctor, and will I have to tell my husband how it happened and tell him about this place? I could lose it now, this place. The tentative thread of calmness I have been hanging onto all day has snapped and I start to weep. I will go home later today. I will make dinner and settle the children with baths and stories. I will make conversation with the husband I have come to despise. The cheating, wayward husband who thinks he can buy me with three pieces of silver and tie me to him with the forever debt of children. Robert reminds me every day that it was *me* who wanted the twins, *me* who spent his money, *me* who underwent the trauma of IVF, *me* who nearly died giving birth. But I'm not going home yet.

Waiting anxiously at the doctor's surgery, I keep pressure on the still bleeding cut. The niggling feeling of guilt at having skived off for the day isn't helping. Not one to read the dog-eared, out of date celebrity magazines, I look around me for the distraction of pictures on the walls. A large black and white photograph catches my eye.

The yacht is sailing hard on the wind, all sail up and drawing, the gunwales dipping into the water. Head sail and mainsail deployed, it scythes through the water. With a sizzle of sound the waves move apart. We slice through. Sailing to the new, sailing away, somewhere far away, and free.

It's a beautiful shot and it's the heeling of the yacht that draws my attention. I feel like that sometimes and more often of late. It's a precarious balance. I am that boat. I fear that if I tip too far I'll lose my sanity. My life at the moment is just like that boat. But that boat has a skipper while I'm lost at sea.

I move closer to the photo and notice the signature. *Williams, 2012.* I wonder who it is. Then I see the boat's name. *Allegro.* What a coincidence. It is aptly named, swift and bright. Under the name-plate I can barely make out some numbers. Oh, how can that be? They match the numbers on the yellow float –*5078*. The name *Allegro* fits the scratched on letters. Could my mysterious key have a connection to this beautiful boat?

I walk toward the receptionist's desk to ask if she knows who owns the boat. I have the key out to show her, but the doctor emerges from his office and invites me in. I put the key on the desk and untie the sopping hankie from my hand. The doctor's name is Brian Williams, new to the practice he tells me. This little clue escapes me. I'm concentrating on my hand, which he cleans and he tells me he'll need to suture it. He keeps glancing distractedly at the key on the table and I realise the link … it's his boat, his key!

Our eyes meet, he is smiling and I am excited.

'This is yours, isn't it?' I ask.

'Where on earth did you find it? I lost it sailing two weeks ago.'

I tell him I was tidying up the place where I play my flute. I keep talking, telling him why I go there, how sad and stuck I feel in my rapidly unravelling marriage. How tired I am, how I don't want to go home. I stop speaking. My words have become a mangle of petulant whining and I am crying. Again. Is there no end to this? I force myself to settle down. I notice the doctor playing with the key.

'What is the key for? Surely your yacht doesn't need such a large one?'

'It's my front door key.'

'Oh.'

Gone the journey through time itself; gone the musical interlude; gone the romantic swords-smith; gone the escape by sea. He's just a week-end sailor with an old fashioned front door key. My hand burns as he finishes stitching. He gives me a tetanus shot. All matter of fact. Tells me I can go home now. Didn't he hear me? I don't want to go home. I tell him this. He pats the back of my good hand.

'Mrs Riley, you will feel better when you're at home with your family.'

I don't believe him.

Plain Jane

Jane McLean

Jane had been priming herself for this night.

For three months, 2 weeks and 5 days to be exact. Ever since she sent back the RSVP with a tick in the 'Able to Attend' box.

She talked to herself as she walked up the stairs, pausing for breath, then a final reminder, her usual self-talk.

'It's OK. These people are old school friends.'

Jane repeated the word 'old' and cringed. That's when her knees felt weak and her mouth went dry.

One step, a second step and there she was at the doorway looking into the brightly ballooned and streamered room, the old school colours of blue and yellow. Such a dynamic combination for a bathroom décor, but tonight the colours only served to remind her of why she was here. The 20 year high school reunion - and she was just about to step into a room full of strangers. Not school buddies, or chums or friends. Just 100 or so strangers moulded together in their competitive finest, small talk, ramblings of children, achievements, marital statuses, residential locations and career titles.

'Great! I am husband-less, child-less, almost home-less, recently mother-less and soon to be job-less,' Jane murmured to no-one in particular. "Why am I doing this?'

She hadn't re-invented herself, so why bother going back into the past, to people she barely knew, those who knew so little about her. They didn't care about her much at school so why would anyone pay any attention to her now, twenty years later.

Plain Jane, that's what they called her then. Right around the time that catchy hair colouring television ad. 'Plain Jane…but not anymore' cooed the voluptuous model on the TV, as her long golden locks swished and sashayed around her blemish-free face. Sales of the product went through the roof, but the plain Janes without stunning blonde hair suddenly became painfully aware of their inferior status and were socially scarred.

For Jane, already bearing the 'Jane' moniker, the 'Plain Jane' label stuck. And stuck well.

Even a new marital surname hadn't altered her first name, or the taunts that went with it. 'My plain Jane' from the now ex-husband, 'our plain Jane' from friends and parents. Plain and ordinary, and mostly invisible. That was how Jane felt about Jane.

Her stilettoed shoes suddenly felt about as glamorous as gumboots, weighing her down.

Once inside, Jane scoured the room for just a hint of recognition. She knew *she* wouldn't be recognised. There was no expectation of immediate rushing over to greet her, with hugs and air kisses and subsequent gushing conversation about her uninteresting life.

Jane decided she would be happy to find a circle – any circle of people, offering token integration with minimal expectation to contribute! In reality, she just wanted to blend in without any fuss. But no-one welcomed her.

No-one was even aware of her presence in the room. Fight or flight. Jane contemplated the latter, with a dignified exit of course.

Teetering in high heels and desperate to find balance both in her shoes and her head, she weighed up her options - force her way into the groups with a fake beaming smile, or continue to stand by herself, stage left, like an accountant trying to do stand up comedy at a basement club. No laughs, no applause, just incredibly alone ... and a failure. She giggled, visualising the accountant wearing a brown cardigan, checked shirt, bow-tied, in tweed cuffed trousers, holding a briefcase with a single banana inside.

Another giggle escaped. Jane suddenly realised she was actually enjoying her own company. Several people look around to source these mini laughter noises.

Then, an incredibly handsome man, tall with sandy sun-bleached hair strode towards her.

'Is that you, Jane? You look great. It's me, Steve. You probably don't remember me ... English - Miss Bronson, Maths - Mr Mitchell.'

Here she stood, in front of the boy she had loved with unrequited devotion for six long and miserable high school years. The school captain and football hero, the boy who stole her ruler in Maths class.

'I think I still have your ruler' he began.

'Oh yeah, that's right. My weapon of maths instruction,' she blurted out, then laughed tentatively at her own joke.

Steve's eyes glistened as his voice flowed like symphonic music to her ears. He joined her in laughter - louder, louder until both of them were nearly doubled up in side-splitting, jaw-aching pain. Others are drawn into the moment, as Steve repeats the joke to the circled audience. The laughter becomes contagious. Not at her, but with her. Strong arms steered Jane to a quiet corner. 'Wait here. Don't move.'

Steve returned with two glasses of champagne. His fingers

lightly touched her hand, sending yummy tingles down her back, her knees and into her toes.

Cupping her face gently in his hands, Steve looked deep inside her soul and whispered, 'You are just as beautiful now as you were in school.

Plain Jane? Not anymore.

An inconvenient client

Louise Elizabeth

My phone beeps at me, as I hurtle down Macquarie Street and into the Domain car park. I grab my briefcase, sling my handbag over my shoulder and head for the nearby Court.

I sound like a train as I try to catch my breath and slide into a seat behind the bar table. I glance at my mobile and my heart contracts as I see David has rung again.

No time for the lift. I dash down the internal courthouse steps, hoping my case wasn't called while I've been doing a plea in the courtroom upstairs. As I wave to my anxious client and walk inside, the Court officer intones my matter. The judge smiles.

'Ms Hindmarsh, good to see you could fit us into your busy schedule.'

A fresh-faced colleague sniggers.

Deadpan, I reply, 'Your Honour, I always have time for matters before you.'

His eyes crinkle. We've had this conversation many times. It isn't as though he doesn't understand what it's like in private practice. His memory must go back more than the five years he's been on the bench, but I suppose he has to exercise his authority and distance himself from former colleagues.

My client is happy.

'You're worth every cent. I can't tell you how pleased I am.'

'Thanks. Don't forget to tell your friends.'

Another satisfied client. I get the usual warm glow from a job well done. What is it they say about pride…?

I look around but my heart contracts as I remember there is no Charles Dittwater to have an easy chat with about my case, or his, or share the latest gossip. His death was so sudden, leaving many unanswered questions.

Back at the office, I bask in the praise of my secretary, Suzie Templar, and clerk, Peter Smythetone. The contract dispute I had successfully handled, not only brought in good fees, but would help to raise my profile in civil litigation. I want to diversify from the usual Family Law and criminal clients. My partner has been dropping hints that it might be time for me to hand these matters over to more junior solicitors. Peter is nearly through his final exams, and will be admitted this year. Suzie tells me that she is ready to resume her studies, and so should be admitted in a couple of years, barring any more hiccups. I feel good.

Back to reality, and the pile of files on my desk. Time passes quickly as I sort out clients' problems. Unfortunately, it's easier to deal with them rather than my own.

I berate myself for feeling sorry for myself, after yet another call from my soon to be ex, David Gruntley. That man drives me up the wall: saps my sense of wellbeing with his unrelenting whinging, and hassling about money. Seven calls a day is unreasonable and draining. The deterioration in our relationship bewilders me. What happened to his *undying love*? I know my settling for second best wasn't the greatest solution, but it was a solution. Serves me right for marrying a businessman. Should have stuck with the professions. At least I understand their ethics. *Will I never be free of that bad choice?*

My moods lightens as I remember the lawyer David has picked charges fashionably high fees notwithstanding it's a pity about his knowledge of the law.

With exaggerated care, I put down my phone, sit back and look past the jumble of files, out the window, and across the harbour, towards the Sydney cityscape. Dark clouds are gathering over the skyline, and it seems a storm is brewing.

I feel a shiver of energy run up and down my spine. Just what I don't need. *I hope this isn't an omen.* I thought things were getting back on track. First Charles dies, and now David thinks he knows more about the law than I do. They say things come in threes. I wonder what's next. Winning lotto? *As if.*

A knock on the door cuts short my musing, and Suzie announces, 'Meredith, Jonathon Blackhook's here.'

I'm jerked back to work. 'Who?'

'You know – the financier. He doesn't have an appointment.' She looks over her shoulder. 'He said Charles referred you to him, but he wouldn't tell me what it's about.'

My heart contracts. 'Charles? How could he refer anyone? He's dead.'

Suzie raises an eyebrow at my emotional response. 'I know but that's what he said.' She starts to back out of the room. 'I told him you had another appointment in ten minutes, but he said that was all he needed.'

'Okay.' I give into the inevitable. 'Show him in. I'd like you to stay and give me a reminder when the time's up.'

I straighten my workspace, put on my grey suit jacket, and walk to the side of the desk. A forty-something man with lightly greying hair, blue eyes, and a slim body enters my office. His tall frame sits easily in his pinstripe suit, its cut showing the hallmark of a tailor-made. The little logo on his shirt is a replica of my late father's - obviously made in the same place. He holds an attaché case, and extends his right hand. I shake it, and lean my shorter body against my solid mahogany desk.

'Thank you for agreeing to see me, Ms Hindmarsh. I won't take up too much of your time.'

He looks mournful, but he doesn't fool me; his eyes are cold and watchful. I wonder how often he practises that look. I wait.

'When I first transferred my business to Charles Dittwater, he told me if I was ever in trouble, and he wasn't available, to come and see you.'

I notice his smile doesn't reach his eyes.

'He said you were like a terrier.'

I force a smile into my eyes. It took me ages to perfect this. My way of being friendly when I don't feel like it. They say, 'fake it 'till you make it''. I'm not getting good vibes from this man.

'How can I help you?'

'My son, Danny, got mixed up with people I'd call the wrong crowd. The police say he's involved in an import duty scam and the detectives say he confessed.'

'If he's confessed, then I'm sorry, but it sounds like a plea to me. He gets a sentence discount for an early guilty plea.'

Jonathon Blackhook holds up an elegant hand. I admire his manicure.

'The police allege he's been altering the classification of goods so they appear as second-hand when in fact they are new. Others had to be involved, and the police say there's fraudulent behaviour by Danny, and his staff, and, apparently, some of the Customs people, and even Federal police. It's big.'

He makes it sound so important, as though it had to be something on a sufficiently grand scale for him to worry about it. I understand his son is involved, but he seems more interested in the newsworthiness of the case, rather than how his son will fare. *Oh well. Another one of those publicity-seeking clients.*

'Yes, I read about it in the paper. Charles Dittwater was acting for your son.' I take a step away from my desk towards the door. 'I thought it was a trial. I didn't talk to Charles about it.'

'It is, or rather it has to be. My son's innocent.' Jonathon Blackhook looks down at his fingernails as he continues. 'Tony Jadson – he's the Sales Manager of East West Imports who employed Danny.' His lips thin. 'Tony and I were at university together and he can't speak highly enough of Charles. His death was a real tragedy.' His eyes search mine apparently looking for a reaction. I give none. *Does he really expect me to burst into tears or go into gory details?* He hesitates and then continues. 'I'm really worried. I want to get Danny the best representation I can.' He subjects me to his hangdog expression. 'I hope you can help me.'

My last big case came to an abrupt end when my long-time client made a run from the court, and wound up under the wheels of a semi-trailer on its way to Macquarie Street to join a truck protest. It made a big splash in the papers. So Jonathon Blackhook is right, I do have some time but not a lot...

(an excerpt from Louise's debut novel *Meredith Isn't Amused*; a crime thriller)

Cracker Night at Wombarra Heights

Jo Hanrahan

It would soon be Cracker Night up in the bush at Wombarra Heights. For weeks, the neighbours had been collecting firewood and dumping it on Harrison's Green in readiness. Everyone would be there – Who could miss the best night of the year? Cracker Night. The pile of wood was getting bigger every day. Soon it would be as big as Harrison's house.

Excitement was in the air. This year it was to be more spectacular than ever before. Fathers were stocking up on crackers for the fireworks, and mothers were making sure the potato box was full of spuds. Anyone knows you can't have a Cracker Night without spuds. As the day drew near, the woodpile for the bonfire grew even higher.

As twilight gathered, people began to arrive. Stinky Aston was the first to arrive; followed y 'Bruiser' Lenham and 'Dummy' Harris – all carrying bundles of kindling. Dummy couldn't speak or hear, but that didn't bother him – he enjoyed himself just the same. And everyone liked him. Boxes of crackers were dumped on his mother's veranda by Georgy Harrison and a few of his mates.

Kids came from everywhere. The bush kids wouldn't miss Cracker Night for quids. They had talked of nothing else for weeks. Mickey Myerscoff, from across the gully came early. Tommy and Teddy Potts, and Jackie Harris from over near the sawmill came together.

Jackie's mate, young Phil Owen, tramped up the road. Stocky young Albert Anilzark strolled nonchalantly down the bush track nearby. Lanky 'Squeaker' Dodds, little 'Bluey' DeCluet and smart Darby Ranger converged from opposite sides of The Green. 'Tiddy' and 'Tubby' Parkinson, the terrible twins, slunk over after dark to ogle the girls. Sexy Violie Ashton peered around at the boys as she glided onto The Green in her tight, slinky dress. 'Pommy' Gray, with his sisters Velie and Josie, came quietly to the sidelines. 'Eggy' Vigal had come up along the main road to meet with his girlfriend, Blondie Hindmarsh, who lived across the paddock. He's been sweet on her for ages. She arrived with a big bag of spuds; blonde hair in a perfect pageboy, sleek as ever.

Darkness fell. Amid cheers and shouting the fire was lit. Flames shot heavenward – raging higher and higher. Smoke billowed ominously. Mrs Harrison, whose house fronted The Green, began to look worried.

Whoosh went the rockets. Zing went the Catherine Wheels.

And everywhere could be heard the Pop! Pop! of the Tom Thumbs. All the while the kids of the bush squealed in delight. Gradually, as the chill settled in over The Green, the fire started to die down. There wasn't much wood left to feed it.

Eventually all the fireworks were gone, the bungers collected and refired as fizzers. The lost ones would be found in the morning. The firewood had burned down. Embers glowed. This was the next highlight of the evening. Where were the spuds? The bushes parted as the small children crept back with bags and boxes of spuds raided from their mother's pantries.

Then, the real fun began.

Stomachs rumbled as spuds turned black among the embers. Garden forks and rakes – anything that wouldn't burn – were called into service to drag those little black beauties from the almost spent ash of the fire. The delicious smell of potato flesh rose as crusty skins were broken to reveal their snowy white insides.

The feast lasted into the wee hours of the morning. Sated and relaxed, everyone agreed that this years' Cracker Night was the best yet. The cleanup could wait until tomorrow.

Drawing the Line

Mary Gabb

Ernest Bland had life sorted out at a very young age. When he left school he was sent to a Weet-Bix Factory to earn a living. One day as he lifted a Weet-Bix packet to put the footy cards inside, he injured his back. He howled with pain, and could not lift another packet of Weet-Bix. So he quit.

No more stupid time-sheets, no more smelly Weet-Bix, no, no he would certainly draw the line at that! Doctor after doctor could find nothing wrong with him, but at last an elderly practitioner was found who agreed.

'Yes, indeed you do have a very bad back Mr Bland!' From that day on, if he could help it, Ernest never worked another day in his whole life.

However he did enjoy a round of golf on Sunday mornings with his mates, and on summer afternoons he would even join them for a game of tennis. Sometimes on a very hot day, with his friends he would end the day with a swim at Brighton Beach. Those were the days.

As his mates gradually disappeared for more serious things, Ernest got lonely. After a long absence he decided to go back to Church. Lingering after Church one day a young girl with flashy auburn hair, engaged him in conversation. Before too long she was sitting beside him in Church, inviting him out to lunch and including him in young people's outings. Several years passed and then, without him quite knowing how it happened, there was suddenly a Mrs Ernest Bland clinging to his arm.

Mrs Bland was determined to fix Ernest's back one way or another, and to send him off to work as soon as possible. But in the meantime she had a good job as a cook, and lucky Ernest happily whiled away his time at home. It was very nice having someone to fuss over him, to do his washing, to make bountiful breakfasts, luscious lunches and delicious dinners for him.

Mrs Bland drew the line at nothing that would save them money; she even cut Ernest's hair and sewed pyjamas for him. Very nice pyjamas they were too, with pineapples and coconut trees and blue lagoons on them. It would be so nice she thought to have a tropical holiday together; perhaps the pyjamas would inspire her beloved.

When quite by accident two little auburn-haired girls joined the family, Mrs Bland took on a second cleaning job at the weekends. She prayed every day that dear Ernest's back would get better, and that he would be able to go to work.

'I do wish you would find a job, Stinky dearest,' she said sweetly. 'We could have a nice holiday with the two girlies.'

I've got an idea Sweet Pea,' replied Ernest, 'I'll build a catamaran and then we can all sail off to a tropical island for the holiday of your dreams.'

Mrs Bland was silent. She could not imagine Ernest with his bad back building even a sand-castle! Soon Ernest found some catamaran plans in a book he got from the public library, and started to buy timber and glue and nails out of Mrs Bland's housekeeping money.

Over the years the catamaran took shape, until a huge whale-like skeleton filled the back yard. He invited the boat building inspector to have a look at it. The inspector looking very solemn, hemmed a bit and slapped an 'Unauthorized' notice on it. Earnest had deviated from boat building regulation Number 1751Z, he pronounced severely. 'Anyway,' he said, 'how do you think you could get it out of your back yard? You would have to demolish your house to do that!'

Ernest scratched his head thoughtfully, and promptly gave up his dream to take his family for a nice tropical holiday. Mrs Bland prayed even harder. 'Dear God, I'm tired of working so hard. Make poor Ernest's back better so he can get a job and look after us properly!'

'I've got an idea!' announced Ernest one fine summer day. 'I could make a mint of money if I turned our little car into an open tourer.' The family car was a 1970 model red VW, and the thought of it with its top cut off was quite a pleasant one.

'How will we manage without a car?' asked Mrs Bland anxiously.

'It won't take me long,' Ernest replied, 'then we can sell it and buy another one.' So in the blinking of an eye Ernest got out his power tools and sliced the top off the little red VW.

'It's got to have roller bars,' said the car compliance inspector, 'otherwise you can't register it. And I won't issue a 'Compliance Certificate' until it is fixed.'

It was all too hard for poor Ernest, and the little red topless VW sat in the yard together with the whale-like structure which should have been taking them on a long sea voyage.

Now Mrs Bland had to catch the bus every day to work and walk to the corner store for her groceries. By this time her beautiful red hair was greying, she had lost the sparkle in her eyes and the spring in her step. Every day she went past the corner store, she bought a chocolate bar to comfort herself.

You silly old goat, she thought, *I don't believe you have a sore back at all!* After she had done the dishes all by herself one night she exploded, 'Stinky dearest, I'm tired of working my fingers to the bone, while you are doing nothing but thinking of crazy schemes all day long. If you don't get a job soon, I'm quitting work!'

'I've got an idea,' he replied. 'I've been thinking of it for some time now. I think I will go into making coffins!'

'Coffins, my goodness, whatever for?' exclaimed Mrs Bland.

'Well, I can use the timber from the catamaran in the back yard, and it won't cost a cent,' announced Ernest.

He was very proud of himself for thinking of such a clever idea. His hair by now had nearly all gone, and what was left was snowy-white. He had white whiskers growing out of his nose and his ears, and his cheeks and nose were very pink. His back was bent and his tummy stuck out in front. He wheezed when he walked and his movements were slow. The Girlies had grown up, left home and were now living as far away as they could.

'I know what, I'll make you one first,' he said. 'Then I'll have it ready when it is needed, and what a lot of money I will save.' He beamed proudly.

When the coffin was ready for finishing Ernest shouted, 'Come here Sweet Pea. I want you to try it out for size. Just hop in and we'll see if it's a good fit.' So Mrs Bland obediently hopped in.

It was a very tight fit since the chocolate bars that she had eaten to comfort herself every day had gone straight to her hips. Mr Bland had to push and squeeze her in, and eventually he got the spade to lever her in around the hips. He was very red in the face when he had finished, and Mrs Bland was squashed in so tightly that she couldn't move.

'Let me out,' she shouted, 'this time you really have crossed the line! I don't want your silly coffin; you and your stupid ideas!' She popped like a cork out of a champagne bottle, fizzing with rage. She took a Mars bar from her pocket and started to unwrap it to comfort herself.

'Mrs Bland, don't eat that chocolate bar!' Ernest commanded loudly. 'You'll never fit!'

At that, Mrs Bland cracked. She whopped Ernest on the head with the garden spade, picked up her purse and put on her best hat. 'Cook your own bountiful breakfasts, luscious lunches and delicious dinners. I'm going to live with the girlies in Darwin!' she announced angrily.

And she did!

More about Harry

Linda Brooks

Truth, they say, is stranger than fiction. On impulse I went through my memory box to look at the war medals entrusted to me by my beloved Uncle Gordon Stockdale ('Gorgie'). There are two sets of medals there - his and those of another. I look at his regularly, but I focused on the ones belonging to the man he'd fought beside, a man he described as 'closer than a brother'; Harry.

Harry had married Gordon's sister, making him my uncle and Gordon's brother in law. I tried to decipher the Service Number on the back of the medals. I wanted to know if I had remembered the story correctly. And I wanted to know more about Harry. After a few failed attempts at identifying him through The Australian War Memorial site, I found him.

He was born in Cheshire, England, the son of William who had left at some time for Canada. He was the son of Lucy, a woman forced to become the head of her small family not long after Harry's birth. She is listed as a dressmaker and an independent earner. At that time she had Harry, 3 and Emily, 6. She emigrated with the two children, settling in Sydney.

Harry died during the war so I only had Uncle Gordon's stories to form a picture of Harry. I don't know how it came to be that his medals were in Uncle Gordon's keeping. I only know they were given to me many years before 'Gorgie' died. He'd told me many stories over the years and the story of his friendship with Harry captured my young heart.

I'd never met Harry, so I couldn't explain the tingling anticipation I felt as I searched the internet for evidence, for more information. The medals told part of the story - 'The Africa Star', 'The Australian Defence Medal' and 'The 1939-1945 Star', along with three round silver medallions with King George IV's profile. They are attached to a brass bar with a combination of awkwardness and care that speaks of both pride and ingenuity. I wondered whose hands had stitched them there. Uncle Gordon's medals were simply held with safety pins - over all the years he never bothered to mount them in any way, although he wore them every Anzac Day, along with Harry's. He'd been a member of the 4th AUST FD AMBULANCE.

I found Harry's story. It was also the story of the 2/17 Australian Infantry Battalion. It was the story of battlefields in Africa, Syria, Lebanon and Tobruk - of years of fighting without end. Harry had joined in 1940 so when he returned to Australia in the summer of 1943 he was a warrior. He married my aunt that year. Her shining face from the photo frame flits through my mind as she walked with carefree steps down George Street in Sydney.

I cradled the medals, feeling blessed to have more than a memory of my uncle's words - I had a love story, and a story of brotherhood. Shortly after marrying my aunt, Harry was sent with his battalion to Papua, New Guinea. There he was joyfully reunited with his best friend, Lance Corporal Gordon Stockdale.

He lived and fought there only a few short weeks, and is buried in the Lae War Cemetery. I looked at the date of his death. I can't begin to describe the feeling. He died on the October 10, 1943 and I was sitting holding his medals on the same date, 70 years later.

The Bachelors and Spinsters Ball

Jane McLean

HER STORY

Another year, another B & S Ball. 'Bachelors and Spinsters' are such derogatory labels for victims of dramatic divorces, spiteful separations, messy marriages. Three hundred people crammed into the auditorium eager to exorcise the past.

And those stupid lucky door prizes, meagre consolation for those luckless in love.

The MC slowly opens the envelope, his eyes darting around the room to gauge attention. He steps closer to the microphone almost swallowing it, grinning broadly to his captive audience.

Reaching the depths of lung capacity, he delivers an extravagant announcement in a rich 'n creamy radio voice, 'Ladies and Gentlemen - The Prize – Two return plane tickets to anywhere in the whole wide world.'

Indifferently I sip my champagne, willing the next prize to be announced.

My Prize, the twin carb, turbo, auto ignition Laser Lawnmower with catcher and mulcher.

Lauded as 'every man's dream machine', mine because I do every man's work since Bill ran off with Suzanna with a 'z', the bottled blonde floozy who used to live next door.

A hushed room. Time stands still. Each person mouthing their own name.

Mr MC clears his throat... 'The winner is ... Jenny Jones.'

Who?

Shocked gasps from my fellow diners, hand patting, back slapping, token gestures to the woman who stole their prize.

But what about the lawnmower? *My lawnmower.*

Unsteadily I get to my feet, heavily weighted by taking something I didn't want, I didn't need.

Smiling sweetly with false excitement I relieve him of the sacred envelope, hear the thunderous applause and race back to my table to figure out my options.

Big decisions to make ... tomorrow.

Flicking over the tickets, my eyes take in the fine print, obviously 6.1 font: *Cannot be redeemed for cash. Cannot be sold, swapped or given to a friend. Cannot donate. Must be taken within 24 hours of issue date.*

Issue date? The answer requires closer inspection of the tickets. There it is, neatly dressed in red ink.... Date stamped... yesterday... 10pm.

Big decisions to make. *Now.*

Where to go? Who to take? What to wear? Why me? My jumbled thoughts are all clamouring for the right to be heard.

'Thanks everyone for a great night. You really cheered me up.' Teeth gritted behind my grin. 'Gotta get to the airport.' Pausing for breath, 'Tonight I will be on a big jet airliner going anywhere I want.' Then I nail it in a little deeper with 'while you all just go back home.'

It felt great to get that off my chest to the miserable, shallow group of condescending, patronising wannabe couples. All those knights in tarnished armour wrestling with tainted maidens in waiting. Dressed in ballooning ball gown and tenuous stiletto sandals, sticking out amongst the Fitzroy Street crowd like a hitchhikers thumb, I flag down the silver service cab and hit the Tulla Freeway, via quick enroute stop at the house. It used to be a home, when Bill was there. Now, it's just a house. I desperately wanted that homey feel back again (minus Bill of course) and I truly believed my own lawnmower would do the trick. Women mowing lawns is a flagrant disregard of co-dependency, a public declaration of their inbuilt coping mechanism.

No time to change; just grab the passport, cram essential items into the overnight bag and turn off the lights. Goodbye house. I turn to call out goodbye to Bill and stop mid-sentence. He's gone … he left me … for her…

Tiring of being bitter and insular, consumed by what ifs and post mortems, I make a snap decision to banish Bill from my thoughts forever, washing my hands of the marriage that once was.

Yessiree! I'm free! The blonde with a 'zee' can have Bill who's a 'b'. A giggle escapes, and I am actually skipping down the path.

Snuggling into the soft leather seat of the cab 'International please'. I close my eyes to give myself time to think, to rest, to process everything logically.

Tullamarine *Aeroporto Internazionale* here I am, making it sound exotic in my own mind on the pretext that I will be arriving in Roma, Italy sometime tomorrow.

'Thirty five dollars lady.'

'Grazie,' I reply, surprising even me.

A mad dash to the counter, my overnight bag swinging wildly bashing into anything slow moving or under four feet. Out of breath, I am in front of a young uniformed lady whose breasted badge states 'Samantha', such a bewitching name. She is staring, mouth gaping, trying desperately to recall training that covered this situation. Her face registers blank.

I put her out of her misery; hand over my passport, the tickets, feeling the sudden need to justify my appearance.

'I won the prize at the Singles Ball tonight.'

Exhale.

'So put me on the next available flight out of here, please and thank you.' A few false nail clicks on her keyboard, then young Samantha sheepishly states, 'Casablanca, Morocco.'

I fake bravado with 'Say it again, Sam.' I need her to clarify the destination! I was actually thinking more along the lines of Italy, if it has to be far away. Alternatively, Fiji, Bali or Vanuatu would be fine... they're close by... safe. Safe is smart, right?

Without prompting, my right brain kicks in and echoes 'tonight is the night my imagination takes flight.... takes flight.... takes flight'

'Casablanca. Of all the gin joints, in all the towns, in all the world I had to land in this one.' My obscure attempt at humour.

Samantha remains nonplussed. 'Madam, there are two tickets here. Is anyone accompanying you?'

It's difficult to figure she is insinuating that I am old, decrepit and in need of a carer or simply stupid, childish and in need of a grown up, or perhaps a combination of some of the above.

I survey the departure crowd farewelling family, friends, loved ones; the tears, the hugs, the kisses.

'You tell me,' I tell her.

'Wait!' I halt her thoughts midstream. 'The other person, do they have to go to the same place?'

Her stare (it's really a glare) takes in my glamour outfit and I know she is plotting her revenge by giving me seat allocation 65B, stuck in between ten-tonne Tessie and a boozy teenager.

'No. They are both open tickets to anywhere.'

I spot the mischievous twinkle in her eyes.

Samantha, my new BFF, has forgiven me for two serious offences: my inappropriate dress sense when travelling; the other, my inane questions that challenge her customer service skills. Her whole face lights up as she owns the mission I have handed her, scanning the huddles of those waiting to board affectionately intertwined with those who will be left behind.

'There – that group.' She points to an elderly man, grey haired, doddery, who is sobbing openly as he mouths 'I love you' to two generations locked in possibly their final embrace, clearly his daughter and her child.

We signal him. He potters over, wiping his eyes with the back of his hand.

United we tell him our plan.

His hug crushes us both, his boyish delight lingering in my heart. You sweet old man, you deserve this.

Jolted from the moment, hearing another rich 'n creamy radio voice: 'Final call for Emirates Flight EK407 to Casablanca, via Dubai. We welcome our First Class Passengers now boarding at Gate 21.'

No fond farewells for this adventure-bound gal.

I saunter to the gate singing at the top of my voice, *'I'm leaving on a jet plane - Don't know when I'll be back again.'*

Another year, another birthday.

Today is my day, my birthday party. 80 for god's sake. In my 81st year.

Why didn't Lily take that into consideration when she delivered her surprise? Everyone gushing and ooohing over some hairbrained idea. I need them here. Not over there. Who shuts shop and moves to another country anyway. What's wrong with just staying put?

Believe you me; I will remember this day until I can't remember where my pyjamas are or when to pee.

I put on my crestfallen face and wait for Lily to notice. She doesn't. Instead she justifies it further with 'Kind of a creative sabbatical, Dad. Just Kassie and I,' and then to defend the move added, 'It's only a four hour flight, you know.'

I knew that! Everyone assumes I am old and doddery, but I'm not. I'm not old because I don't feel old. I am certainly not doddery because I still have all my faculties; they're just slowing down, that's all. I hear key words of conversations. I don't dribble. And I dress myself.

Last birthday, I overheard one of the grandchildren snicker 'Mum says that Grandfather Harry is a pain in the ass.' Kids of today. They should be seen and not heard.

Jean had always covered for me with the family by saying 'that's just his way.'

Oh Jean, my rock, my anchor. Lily had been my mainstay for nearly a decade since Jean's passing. The sorrow of losing my wife of forty-five years was eased somewhat by my daughter's maternal presence. And her cooking. Whilst I wasn't overly fussed with Lily's mealtime concoctions, with all those unusual ingredients, (natural she called them, raw crap to me), a home cooked meal sure tasted good regardless of what it was called, and what went into it. Jean was a meat and three veg woman, Sunday roast cooking nicely while we went to church. Fish and chips on Wednesday night; the local Club for fancy dining out.

I enjoyed Lily's company. We would chat about so many things, and sometimes I'd even let her win at scrabble! Now I'm talking in past tense as if they have already left. They can't leave. I need more time with Lily, there are so many things I haven't told her yet, things that should be said before I become a dear departed. So much unfinished business...

Lily is my precious daughter. Named after Jean's favourite flower; the ones Jean carried on our wedding day all those years ago. With Kassie it was, well… different. Her arrival into this world made me a grandfather. For the first fifteen years, feelings for my first grand daughter were borne out of a sense of duty.

Then when Jean became ill with the dreaded 'C', I began to see Kassie in a different light. She would spend hours with her beloved Grandma, chatting incessantly about boys, school, clothes, boys, music, art, boys...

Jean loved that in her grandchildren...the sharing, the laughter, the chin wags.

I would have preferred a grandson. Jean used to say I needed to be more receptive to the love of one's family. 'Being selfless opens up our hearts, Harry' she would scold in her calm Methodist trained voice. I'd just reply with my trademark grunt.

Often wondered why I felt that bond with my daughter and not with the sons. And don't get me started on the ex son-in-law, Kassie's geographically removed father. Waste of space he was. A true oxygen thief.

I digress. Anyways, about Kassie, try as I might in those days, I liked her but I couldn't really say that I loved her, all mushy and stuff.

At Jean's memorial service everything changed. Kassie stood proud and tall, her golden hair all ribboned. She wore the long hippy-looking dress, purples, pinks, yellows, blues and oranges. I'd seen her in that dress before, often when she visited Jean. Don't know why, but my mind wanders as I see all the colours of the rainbow ... just like Jean's basket full of skeins of knitting wool. Jean called it the 'dancing dress'. Kassie said it symbolised the love between Grandmother and Granddaughter that knew only brightness and magic. There she was with Jean's treasured violin perched patiently on her shoulder, waiting to be stroked and plucked, bow poised mid-air.

Kassie searches the packed home of her Grandmother's faith and her eyes make contact with those of her Grandfather, boring deep into my soul. All I hear are heavenly sounds of Amazing Grace. Jean's favourite hymn. I release a throaty 'hrrmpff' in a poor attempt cover up a teary sniffle, and at that moment, I knew. I loved Kassie more than life itself and, in spite of all my short comings, Kassie loved me, her Grandfather Harry.

And so it began, three generations together sharing 'Celebration Days' where Lily and Kassie would choose picnics, bushwalks, browsing bookstores, bike rides. Didn't much go for the bicycle rides! So we didn't do those again! Grandfather Harry days were my choosing. Saturday morning garage sales, a spot of fishing, antique shops or watching the AFL on the television.

Ahh yes, those were the good times. There I am, talking in past tense again. Have to face reality. Them over there, me over here, of course our celebration days are over.

I must have nodded off. Damn heating! Packing up my reminiscences, jolted back to the present with the family 'wowing' and 'whooping'.

Who spiked the punch... the little scoundrel, one of those unruly grandchildren I bet.

'Hey Pop. What do you think about that for your birthday present?' A man's voice. One of the sons.

'Good... Good... yes... Good.' I am helpless. I have no idea what he or anyone else for that matter is referring to. My eyes desperately seek out Lily, or Kassie. And when I am at the point of realising I've totally lost my marbles, Lily's hands are on my shoulders and the sweet scent of Kassie's perfume is close by. I am safe again.

'What's all this kerfuffle about?' trying to sound semi lucid.

'Oh, Grandfather Harry, you must have had a little power nap,' teases Kassie.

'Dad, it's our birthday present to you.' Lily pauses then kisses me on the forehead as you would a child.

Another son butts in, 'You're going to Melbourne for three days, Pop. Before Lil 'n Kas fly out to the sheep country.'

Third son throws his arms into the air and exclaims loudly 'Don't know why it's for three days. Kas, what did you call it? Celebration days? It all sounds a bit loopy to me.'

I am torn between the pesky son's comments and the excitement of Melbourne. And then I remember the purpose of the gift, a farewell before Kassie and Lily begin their adventure across the straits in New Zealand. The quandary persists even as I hug Lily and Kassie tight (Kassie calls them hugs-without-words, where nothing needs to be said, just be lost in feeling loved, she once explained). All the little sayings come flooding back - I know I will miss them both just as much as I have missed Jean over the years.

The flight is uneventful, prissy hostesses treating me like a freeloading pensioner. Speaking loudly assuming I'm deaf, making wild gestures with their hands to symbolise the exits and the toilets.

Melbourne. What a bustling bothersome city. For her 'celebration day' Kassie chose St Kilda for the markets, the beach, footpath eatery places (café hopping, Kas stated. More like all day grazing). Lily had her mind set on the National Gallery for her special day. (Struth! You call that art!) My day was the MCG, Four 'n Twenty pies and 80,000 people to watch real football.

Three days and nights have passed quicker than my ticker. Saddened by the inevitable I dawdle over the packing. I am inconsolable. I don't want them to go. They are so damn inconsiderate. It's not right that kids leave their own flesh and blood behind. They owe me.

Standing in front of the mirror, I repeat out loud 'they owe me', to no-one and everyone. All of a sudden I see the knotted scowls of bitterness, and hear the loathsome grouch of old age and realise the family is right. I am a pain in the ass.

Oh my goodness gracious me. I am having a kidney-blaster. Kassie told me about them, an 'a-pith-in-me'. You know, when everything becomes crystal clear then you go out and do good works, according to my own reworded definition of some psychobabble. In truth, I owe Lily and Kas much more than they owe me. They gave time, caring, even love and…well, what did I do in return? As usual, I just took and took. Jean was right all those years ago, I have been selfish. All I ever wanted was the best for Lily and Kas, for them to be happy. Not like this old bugger, stale and frightened, angry and alone.

It's evening, for goodness sake, and there are swarms of people buzzing around the airport. Cripes, look at those long queues, and the pushing and shoving, the little bees all in a rush. As the rabble noise disappears into the background, I can't stop hugging-without-words my two beautiful girls. A sudden burst of energy brings forth a thought - *I want to go too*. Not because I am afraid of losing them, but simply I want to feel alive again. I break the without-words rule and say proudly 'I love you' to Lily and to Kassie as tears trickle down my cheeks. They sense my change, and reply with gentle strokes to my face between wiping their own tears.

What now! Rudely interrupted from my moment, I am being summoned by the uniformed woman behind the counter and her ballroom-dancer comrade.

Damn! There must be something wrong with the baggage. Stop! Don't get cranky! The cantankerous old fella has been ousted remember, I remind myself.

Releasing myself out of the hug-huddle with my special girls, I shuffle over, wiping my tears away with the back of my hand. The uniformed one name-tagged Samantha and the ballroom traveller speak gibberish, words that simply do not register. I ask them to repeat. And then finally… oh my… I grasp the situation quite well considering my age. Good Lord! Tonight becomes a grand hug-fest as I do another round with these two sweet ladies. My shuffle becomes springy and I feel fifty again. Methinks Jean has rewarded me for finally getting the gist of family love.

Lily gives me the look of 'What's going on, Dad' and Kassie just smiles. She has quickly cottoned on. I give her a wink and she returns the secret sign. Hiding the ticket behind my back, I await the big announcement.

'Final Call for passengers on Qantas Code Share Flight JQ235 to Auckland. Now boarding at Gate 16.'

'Lily. Kas. That's us! Hope they're showing a family movie on our flight.'

Hundreds and Thousands

Jo Tregellis

Jerome hadn't been to the city for six months but today it was necessary. He liked his home at Wangi Wangi. Watching yacht races was a favourite pastime. He needed a doctor's certificate so that he could resume work. Walking up the steps of the station he felt fear in his stomach. 'Go away,' he muttered, leaning his heavy body against the railing. Up a few more steps. People blurred in his vision, dotting the platform like hundreds and thousands. The attendant drawled out the usual blurb. 'Got to get on it.' Carefully he boarded. Great! An empty seat. He sat down slamming his bum bag against the back of the seat. He grabbed it and pulled it to the front. 'Stupid bag.' Jerome checked the ticket in his shirt pocket. 'Remember where it is, 'he told himself.

The window glass was cool on his face. 'Dunno why it has to be so hot at Christmas time.' Jerome closed his eyes. Just four more stations. He learned them by heart because his mum didn't want him to get lost.

'Tickets, please.' The guard was standing beside Jerome. Panic. A frantic search of the bum bag. 'Come on son.'

'I've got one.' He stood up and felt in his trousers pocket. 'Pocket, pocket.' He remembered his shirt pocket. 'Here it is.'

'Were you trying to be smart?'

'No, I'm not smart.' Perspiration dripped from the end of his nose. The ticket was damp in his hand. The guard moved on. One more station.

Jerome got off the train at Wynyard, up the escalator into York Street. The hot wind slapped his face. 'Go away. I hate wind.'

The doctor gave Jerome the all clear. 'The workshop is shut for Christmas,' Jerome explained.

'Well, then, have a good Christmas and be very fit and well for the New Year.'

'Yes Doctor, Bye Doctor, Thank you, Doctor.'

He decided to walk to Town Hall. He felt pleased with himself, pleased with the Doctor.

Five shopping days to go. The sign in the shop window reminded him that he had not yet bought presents for his mum, dad or sister. Another search of the bum bag revealed a five dollar note and some coins. 'Not enough for shopping.'

'Watta yer got in your bag, mate?' A voice boomed behind him.

'Not much.'

'How much?'

'Some coins.'

'Yeah, well give 'em to me.'

'Why?'

'Because I said so.'

'No.' Jerome was defiant. He ran. The voice overtook him. It belonged to a tall youth with fairish hair and protruding teeth. 'Please go away from me.'

'Please go away from me,' the youth mimicked.

Out of the corner of his eye, Jerome saw a police car stopped at a red light. He pushed the youth as hard as he could and ran to the patrol car. 'Please can I get in? That boy is annoying me. He wants my money.'

'Get in son. Can you still see the boy?'

Jerome peered through the closed window. 'No I can't see him now, there's a lot of people.'

'We'll drive around the block. If you see him tell us straight away.'

There was no sign of the youth and Jerome was set down outside the Town Hall.

'Thank you,' he called back.

The Town Hall clock struck mid-day. It's still early. I think I'll walk to the Queen Victoria building. He arrived as the carollers began *The First Noél*. The music made Jerome feel happier. That robber nearly spoiled my day. On the mezzanine level, Jerome leaned on the rail and feasted his eyes on the Christmas décor. He especially liked the wide, lush, red and green ribbons that fell full length from the ceiling. Crowds of shoppers busied themselves on the floor below like colourful ants on a mission.

'More hundreds and thousands,' Jerome said aloud.

'Well-said young man.' An older woman, smartly dressed in a blue skirt suit was standing beside him.

'Oh thank you lady.'

'Do you like all this rushing around?'

'Sometimes I do and sometimes I don't, but today I like it.'

'Me too. What's your name?'

'Jerome.'

'Mine's Sylvia.'

'Hello.'

'I am going to have lunch. Would you like some?'

'I've only got five dollars.'

'That's alright. It's my shout.'

'Are you a stranger?' Jerome asked tentatively. 'I'm not supposed to go with strangers.'

'We were strangers when we met,' Sylvia explained, 'but we know each other's name now. I will understand if you don't want to.'

'I do. I'm hungry. Let's go.'

They left the Queen Victoria building and found a less busy coffee shop. The Turkish bread open sandwich was delicious. 'I've never eaten that bread before. I like it.'

'Would you like coffee Jerome?'

'I like Coke, Sylvia, please.' Jerome sat back in the small chair and felt important.

'What kind of work do you do, Jerome?'

'I work in the workshop.'

'What do you do in the workshop?'

'I put CD's into the plastic cases. I do it real good. My boss is soon going to let me load the truck and after I might be a supervisor.'

'That's great,' said Sylvia. 'I used to be a radiographer but now I'm retired.'

'I had an X-ray once when I broke my arm. The kids at school wrote their names all over the plaster. I have to go home now Sylvia. My train leaves at 3.15.'

'Did you enjoy your time with me?'

'Yes, I did.'

'Do you know why?'

'I think it was because I felt the same. No one said I was different.'

'Me, too.' Sylvia smiled. 'We were hundreds and thousands.'

'Yes we were. Merry Christmas Sylvia.'

'Merry Christmas, Jerome.'

Who Stole Christmas?

Linda Brooks

Mum and Dad were behaving a bit strange this year. With Christmas just around the corner Bella was very surprised at the lack of preparation.

Her mother, who usually overdid everything, was doing nothing. She showed no sign of illness. She simply couldn't have forgotten – Bella knew this because of the number of times she'd said, 'Oh Bella, *do* give it a rest. Stop nagging.'

No-one had died. There wasn't a 'financial crisis', at least not at their house. Both Bella's parents were too careful for that. They had a squirrel-like ability to save money, even in the hardest times, and Bella was sure they must have enough for 10 Christmases.

However, to all appearances, this year there would be none.

Bella asked for her allowance.

Bella asked everyone what they wanted for Christmas. Politely, of course. After all, perhaps she had slipped off the 'nice' list. It wasn't beyond the realms of possibility.

Bella was apprehensive about Santa's 'naughty and nice' list. Being nice was sometimes hard work.

She had long discussions about Christmas with any friend that visited, making sure one or the other of her parents overheard. But neither of them were saying anything.

Then she pulled out all the stops.

She was nice to her brother.

This alone should have earned her a medal, but it was obvious that all her efforts were going unnoticed. It had been particularly trying as her brother had said, 'Buzz off Sis' every time she tried to get him on side. Apparently he hadn't notice, or he didn't care. After all, he was thirteen.

These were drastic times. Had Christmas been cancelled, or worse still –had someone stolen Christmas? It didn't bear thinking about.

All the times that Bella had felt misjudged or misunderstood by her parents, seemed small in the light of this new problem.

To make things worse, Bella wasn't allowed to go here, she wasn't allowed to go there. No more trips to the outside storeroom or the sheds.

This was more than Bella could take – *added on top of all the things she wasn't allowed to say.* She packed a shoebox, dressed her cat, Mr Sox, and prepared to leave home. She made quite a bit of noise getting things together, especially in the kitchen where she had made tomato and cheese sandwiches.

Nobody noticed.

Nobody cared. She was invisible.

After getting to the front gate with no-one begging her to stay, she had shuffled back inside and unpacked.

Of course, the tree was up. Mum did that on November 30 every year. Unless of course, it was a church day, and then it went up the day after. It had the usual decorations, which had initially been a good sign, even if the angel at the top was a little crooked and Mum hadn't let her fix it.

'Leave things along, Bella,' said Mum.

As marvellous as it was to have a tree, Bella was deeply

disappointed. Why a Christmas tree was only the place to put the toys.

The bad news, of course, is that there were none there. Not a single carefully wrapped one. Nothing to shake, poke or rattle when parental eyes were elsewhere. Nothing to boast about at school. Nothing. Not even wrapping paper.

Bella chewed at her bottom lip with worry. What could she tell her friends? If she made up stories to her friends, she would get it wrong. She usually did when she told things that weren't true. She was a hopeless liar.

If she said that there was a huge box with her name on it, she would surely get a small box with a tiny toy. She would never forget the year that she had told her friends that she thought she was getting a new bike and all she'd been given was a fake Minnie Mouse watch. She hadn't lived down the shame.

There was only one thing to do. If her parents could ignore it, so could she. She would be silent too. This tested her miniscule patience. Her head hurt.

'Mum, I have a headache. Do you have something?' she asked, hoping for sympathy at least.

'What the heck for? Do you think I own a pharmacy?' asked Mum, who was not over-endowed with sympathy, being one who never succumbed to even the slightest dose of sniffles.

Bella offered to run next door and ask Mrs Rudge for a Bex powder. She was renowned for taking one every morning just in case she came down with one.

'What!' said Mum, 'Don't even think about it! If that daft woman wants to slowly poison herself, that's her choice. But no daughter of mine will go down that path if I have anything to say about it. Never heard the like!'

Christmas morning dawned. Bella crawled reluctantly out of bed, stumbling grumpily down the stairs. She arrived at the tree.

The room was filled with oddly shaped parcels, like nothing Bella had ever seen before. The wrapping was off in no time.

There was a doll's pram – handmade by Dad. He'd made a fire-truck, and a dozen other small things for Scott. There were beautiful quilts and doll's blankets that had been handmade by Mum. Suddenly all the late night noises made sense. And not being allowed near the shed. There wasn't a store-bought gift.

Mum and Dad sat beaming at Bella and Scott's joyful squeals. Then they opened the little presents from the children.

Bella grew up and had children of her own. They gathered around for the stories the night before Christmas.

The family put the tree up on November 30 every year, just like when she was a child. And every Christmas Bella and the children made cards and presents for each other. Even the littlest one made something.

Sometimes they made decorations as well as gifts, but every year they made some special things to take to the huge Christmas tree in the shopping centre.

And every year, on the night before Christmas, Bella told them the story of how she had thought that someone had stolen Christmas, but that it had turned out to be the best Christmas of them all.

Published as an illustrated childrens' book, 'Who Stole Christmas?'.

Authors

Linda Ruth Brooks first wrote about growing up in a small coastal town, *An Australian Childhood*. Linda's writing is joyful and poignant. She has written poetry, novels and children's stories. Linda engages the reader with raw humour and courage.

Christina Batey always has a smile on her face. Her style is effortless, whimsical and crisp. She has published a teen novella *Kicker*. With three children and a busy life, free time would be like winning the lottery!

Julie Cochrane has the kind of warmth that permeates on a cold night. Considered, weighing her words and responses, she is also spontaneous. Her words get to the heart of life's experiences.

Louise Elizabeth ventured into novel and short story writing following her retirement as a lawyer and academic. Her novels include *Meredith Isn't Amused* and *Cousin Adrian or the Myth of Love*.

Mary Gabb began putting pen to paper (*her spelling very original*) at age five, when 'incarcerated' in a Crippled Children's Home for 2 years. After being dragged around the world with family, Mary life's experiences and observations are begging to be written down.

Jo Hanrahan has lived a full and colourful life. She has travelled the world, studying culture and language. With her origins firmly grounded in the Australian bush, her writing is uniquely Aussie.

Neridah Kentwell's narratives are carefully crafted and rich with imagery. Drawing on her passion for early Australian history, Neridah has been writing for many years in Hunter Valley magazine *Breathe* and the magazine *Town and Country Farmer*.

Marilyn Linn enjoys writing short stories and poems, some of which have been successful in competitions and been published in Australia, New Zealand, Japan and USA. Marilyn's writing is based on crisp observation and intuition. Her debut novella deals with the surgery and aftermath of burns on a young girl.

Jane McLean has a writing style that draws the reader on a surprising journey. With deft skill, she is as comfortable with fiction as nonfiction. Her humour and characterisation is whip-sharp, and her connection to the narrative is pure charm.

Helen Marshall is an artist of renown. She has just finished her debut teen novel *Pulse* which is a crafted tale of a young women who finds herself through the gift of music.

Victoria Norton's writing is heartfelt, emotional, and engaging. She enjoys writing about the way people interact. Victoria is working on a psychological thriller. She has published a collection of short stories *purple. emerald. gold.*

Rina Robinson has many books to her credit. Her first published short story was for a Truckers' magazine. Her boundless energy and imagination is reflected in her writing. The narrative is crisp and engaging and there is suspense at every turn.

Jo Tregellis is a masterful poet. Her work is measured and enduring. Poetry is as natural as breathing to Jo, and as perfect as a science. Many of her poems have won awards. She has been widely published. Her poetry evokes visual imagery that is clear, fresh, authentic and thought-provoking.

Linda Visman migrated from England as a child. A country girl. Living and teaching in remote areas of Central Australia brought a unique appreciation of life. Her first published novel, set in the 1950s, *Ben's Challenge,* is an evocative tale of a young boy determined to find the truth about his father's death.

www.ingramcontent.com/pod-product-compliance
Lightning Source LLC
Chambersburg PA
CBHW031415290426
44110CB00011B/389